D

Wrapper Rockets
&
Trombone Straws

Wrapper Rockets
&
Trombone Straws
Science at Every Meal

Ed Sobey

Illustrated by Carol Chapin and Charles J. Nappa

**LEARNING
TRIANGLE
PRESS**

*Connecting
kids, parents, and teachers
through learning*

An imprint of McGraw-Hill
New York San Francisco Washington, D.C. Auckland Bogotá Caracas
Lisbon London Madrid Mexico City Milan Montreal New Delhi
San Juan Singapore Sydney Tokyo Toronto

McGraw-Hill

A Division of The McGraw-Hill Companies

©1997 by **The McGraw-Hill Companies, Inc**
Published by Learning Triangle Press, an imprint of McGraw-Hill.

Printed in the United States of America. All rights reserved. The publisher takes no responsibility for the use of any materials or methods described in this book, nor for the products thereof.

pbk 1 2 3 4 5 6 7 8 9 FGR/FGR 9 0 2 1 0 9 8 7 6

Library of Congress Cataloging-in-Publication Data applied for

ISBN 0-07-021745-9

CIP

McGraw-Hill books are available at special quantity discounts to use as premiums and sales promotions, or for use in corporate training programs. For more information, please write to the Director of Special Sales, McGraw-Hill, 11 West 19th Street, New York, NY 10011. Or contact your local bookstore.

Acquisitions editor: Judith Terrill-Breuer
Editorial team: Executive Editor, Robert E. Ostrander
       Book editor, Sally Anne Glover
Production team: DTP operator: Jennifer L. Dougherty
       DTP computer artists: Nora Ananos, Charles Burkhour, Steve Gellert,
        Charles Nappa, Jennifer L. Dougherty
       Indexer, Jodi L. Tyler
Designer: Jaclyn J. Boone   FF96

Dedicated to

Woody and Andrew Sobey

for their inspiration and assistance during

hundreds of hours of testing projects in restaurants.

Contents

Introduction *ix*

1 Pipeline to your lips: straws *1*

2 Coffee chorus,
tea tunes *23*

3 It's in the
bubbles *33*

4 Fork frolics,
spoon sports *43*

5 The splash zone:
place mats *51*

6 Absorbing science: napkins *59*

7 Shake it out,
spoon it on *63*

8 Galloping glasses *71*

9 Kindling candles *79*

10 It's a stick-up *87*

11 Pocket change *95*

12 Dessert trivia *109*

Bibliography *131*

Index *133*

About the author *139*

Introduction

Wrapper Rockets and Trombone Straws grew out of the explorations my family and I have made while waiting for pizza. Our Friday night dining out brought us back together after a week of on-the-go activity. My wife, Barbara, and our sons, Woody and Andrew, and I explored everything within reach or gaze. We made games out of all the materials available, and we became scientific investigators in the best sense of the phrase: The only reward for our research was the joy of the activity and of learning.

Wrapper Rockets and Trombone Straws lays out fun activities that you and your family can try at a restaurant—or in your kitchen. You will find some fun facts to share with each other, but the thing you'll enjoy the most is doing the activities together. The minutes of waiting will melt away, and you will cherish the time you spend asking questions, thinking, laughing, and learning.

If you think science is the stuff that oozes out of textbooks, we hope *Wrapper Rockets* will change your opinion. Science is not a collection of facts. It's an active process that we all use to learn about the world around us. This book is a guide to learning through the scientific process at a restaurant.

Our goal is not to cram you full of facts or to make a rocket scientist out of you. (But if you *are* inspired to become a rocket scientist, please write to us. We would be delighted to know about that.) Our goal is to get families to marvel at the wonders of the close-at-hand. We want families to raise questions, think, enjoy each other's company, and have fun.

The shocking truth is this: Science is fun. If you dig up a fossil while working in the garden or take apart an old appliance or try to make the perfect paper airplane, that's science. You'll raise questions and want to know the answers. You'll form ideas and test them. In your quest to explore, you will encounter problems and solve them. You might ask experts to answer questions or look in an encyclopedia. You'll be using the scientific process and learning.

What do you need to make your dinner a science experience? Your table setting should include some eating utensils, a few straws, salt and pepper, a paper napkin, and a place mat. It would help to have a Swiss army knife, or a small pair of scissors, a few coins, a pencil or pen, and your copy of *Wrapper Rockets and Trombone Straws*, of course.

And when you've tried some of these activities at home or at a restaurant, take this book to your science teacher. Why should you have all the fun and not your classmates, too?

1 Pipeline to your lips: straws

Ask for a straw. Even if you aren't getting something to drink, ask for a straw. They are useful tools for exploring science and having fun. You can make musical instruments, siphon water, launch straw wrappers into orbit, build model bridges, and make small explosions. To do all of these activities, you might want to ask for several straws.

By the way, as you grab a handful of straws, have you ever thought about the materials used to make straws? Years ago, they were all made of paper. Before that, they were made of shafts of wheat or rye. Today most straws are made of polypropylene. That's the same stuff used to make rope, baby bottles, car parts, insulating underwear, and packaging. Polypropylene gives straws strength without much weight. Those qualities make straws great for building and doing a variety of experiments.

Inventing the straw *Marvin Stone invented the paper drinking straw. His motivation to make straws was his desire to make mint juleps taste better. Stone owned a factory that manufactured paper cigarette holders, and he liked mint juleps. Although he liked to drink mint juleps with straws, he didn't like the taste that the rye grass straws gave his drink. So in 1888 he started making straws from paper for his own use. Other people saw him using the paper straws and wanted to use them also. So Stone began producing paper straws at his factory. For 16 years, workers in Stone's factory wound paper around a form and glued the ends to make straws. By 1906, the demand for straws was so great that a machine was invented to manufacture them. The machine eliminated much of the manual labor and made straws cheaper to produce. Stone started a new industry, manufacturing straws, when he solved a simple problem.*

Straw tunes

You can make musical instruments from straws.
It helps to cut the straw, so ask if anyone has
a pair of scissors or a Swiss army knife.

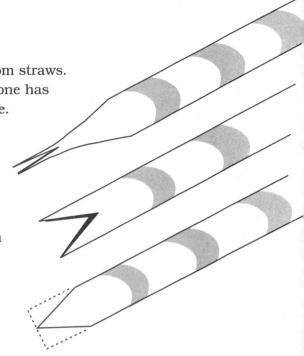

With scissors, cut the edges off one
end of the straw. Starting about
¼ inch from the end of the straw,
angle the scissors to the midpoint
at the end of the straw. Repeat this
on the other side so you are left with
a pointed end. This is the reed of your
instrument. If you can't find scissors,
don't give up. You can still make an
instrument. Just use the flattened
end of the straw as your reed.

Now place the reed between
your teeth. Molars work best.
Chomp on the reed a few times
until it is pliable. Now you are
ready to make music.

Give your tooter a try.
Blow through the reed to make
a steady tone. If no sounds emerge,
it's because the reed isn't vibrating.
Chomp on it a few more times.
Once you have the reed loosened up,
it will vibrate when you blow through
the straw and make a great tone.

Once you have mastered this first straw flute, try varying the design. Take some other straws and cut reeds of different shapes. Do they make different tones?

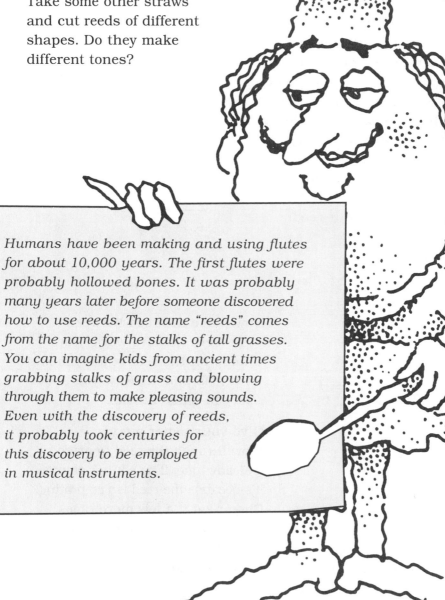

Humans have been making and using flutes for about 10,000 years. The first flutes were probably hollowed bones. It was probably many years later before someone discovered how to use reeds. The name "reeds" comes from the name for the stalks of tall grasses. You can imagine kids from ancient times grabbing stalks of grass and blowing through them to make pleasing sounds. Even with the discovery of reeds, it probably took centuries for this discovery to be employed in musical instruments.

What's happening

As you blow air across the reed, the flowing air pushes the reed up and down. The vibrations of the reed move air molecules back and forth. We hear these vibrations of air and call them sounds. Sounds are vibrating molecules. The vibrating air molecules travel at Mach 1 (the speed of sound, about 1,000 feet per second in air) to your eardrums. Sounds vibrate your eardrums, and the drums transmit the vibrations to your inner ear. Eventually the sound vibrations reach tiny hairs in your inner ears. As the hairs bend, they stimulate nerves that rush the signals to your brain. All that happens in a fraction of a second when you blow on your straw flute.

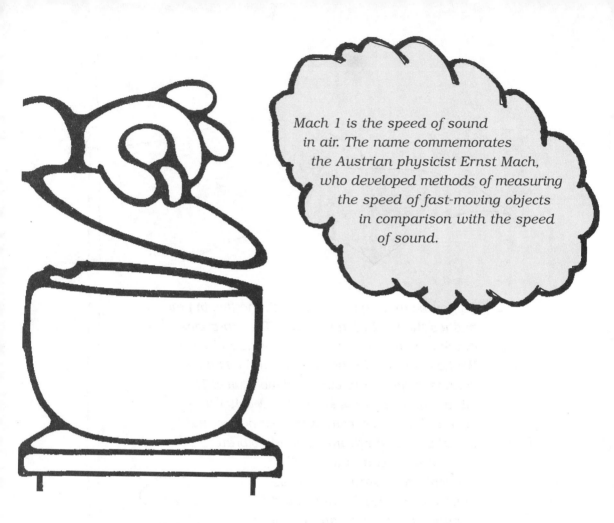

Mach 1 is the speed of sound in air. The name commemorates the Austrian physicist Ernst Mach, who developed methods of measuring the speed of fast-moving objects in comparison with the speed of sound.

The tone of the sound you make depends on the length of the straw. Try cutting an inch or so off the end of the straw. How does the shortened straw sound? Just like the pipes in a pipe organ, the shorter the straw, the higher the pitch. As you shorten the straw, you are shortening the length of the column of air that vibrates. Keep cutting off pieces and listening to the sounds until the straw is so short that you can't make any sounds at all.

If you have a pair of scissors, blow through the straw flute while cutting the straw shorter and shorter. Be careful not to cut off your lips or nose in the process! If you are quick (as well as careful) with scissors and have a large lung capacity, you can make a neat succession of sounds from low frequencies to high.

You can also make your flute longer. Try adding a second straw to your flute. Jam one end of a straw into the uncut end of your straw flute and make some more sounds. Can you make a slide trombone? Wet the end of the second straw and slide it in and out of the straw with the reed. Can you get different tones?
Are you ready for the marching band?

If the restaurant provides flexible straws, you can shorten and lengthen your flute without cutting it. Grab the two ends of a flexible straw. Push the ends together and pull them apart while playing your flute. How many distinct musical notes can you make with a flexible straw?

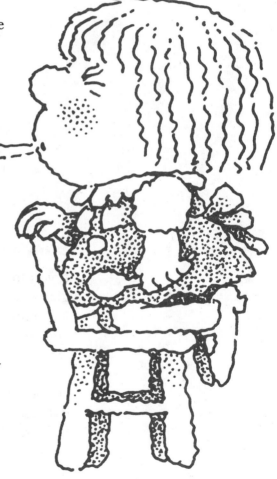

You can also make sounds by blowing across the end of a straw. Hold the straw vertically and blow across the opening. While you are blowing, cover the other end of the straw with a finger. You can get some neat sounds with this reedless flute.

You can vary the pitch of this instrument. Pinch the straw with your thumb and forefinger at different lengths to make different tones. Practice with your instrument, and then belt out your rendition of "Twinkle, Twinkle, Little Star."

Twin-kle, twin-kle, lit-tle star...

By this time, everyone at the surrounding tables will be staring at you. Look confidently back at them and tell them you are conducting an important science experiment. And, in case they ask, tell them yes, you are indeed a rocket scientist.

Blowing sound bubbles

If you tap a spoon on the side of your glass, you get sound at one tone. No matter how hard you whack the glass, you get the same tone. Of course, if you whack it hard enough to crack it or break the glass, you will make a very different sound. However, without doing permanent damage to the glass, you can change the tone by blowing bubbles in your drink.

Ask for some help from one of your companions. While one person blows bubbles through a straw, have the other one tap on the side of the glass. When bubbles are in the drink, the sound has a much lower tone. By controlling when you have bubbles in the drink, you have twice as many tones available from your glass.

*Where did the second tone come from?
Sound moves through air at about
one-fourth the speed that it moves
through water (or milk or soda).
When air bubbles are in the drink,
they slow down the sound waves.
The slower sound has a lower tone.
See what sounds you can create
with other glasses, different levels
of water, and more air bubbles.*

Rockets

If you haven't gotten to know the restaurant staff yet, surely this
experiment will get their attention. Convert your paper-covered straw
into a rocket. Carefully tear 2 inches off one end of the paper wrapper
covering the straw. If you are careful not to jam the other end of the
straw into the paper cover, you are ready to test fire your rocket.

The biggest challenge facing a straw rocketeer is deciding where to aim
the rocket. Good judgment is everything. Select only willing targets,
and make sure their eyes are not endangered. Unwilling targets or an
injury will be the end of your experiments. So think before you launch.

With an enormous puff, you could blow your rocket halfway across the restaurant.

Bad idea.

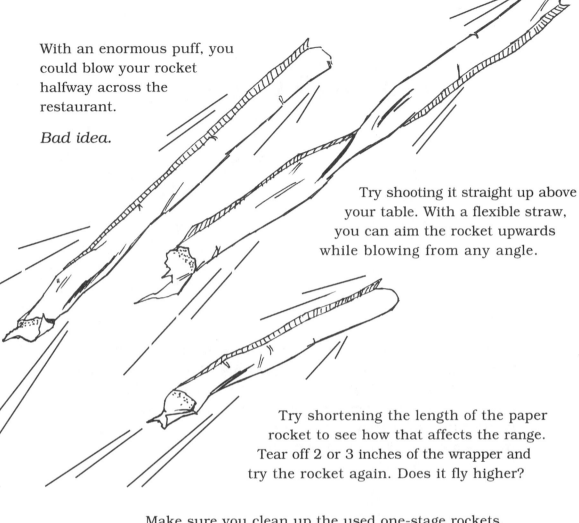

Try shooting it straight up above your table. With a flexible straw, you can aim the rocket upwards while blowing from any angle.

Try shortening the length of the paper rocket to see how that affects the range. Tear off 2 or 3 inches of the wrapper and try the rocket again. Does it fly higher?

Make sure you clean up the used one-stage rockets. Leave no trace of your aeronautical experiments. Rocket scientists are tidy.

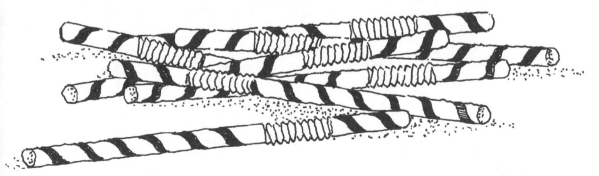

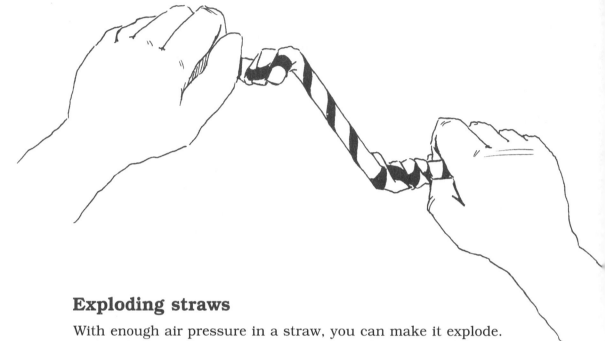

Exploding straws

With enough air pressure in a straw, you can make it explode.
The trick is how to increase the air pressure. Grab the ends of the
straw with the index finger and thumb of each hand. Hold one hand
directly above the other. Now twirl your hands around in a circle,
twisting the straw around itself at each end. It might take you a few
tries before you get the right motion.

What's happening

On the first twist, you are sealing the ends of the straw. With each succeeding twist, you are squeezing the air towards the middle of the straw, increasing the air pressure. When you have wrapped up the straw so your hands are 2 inches apart, the pressure inside the straw could be three or four times atmospheric pressure. With a solid flick of your partner's middle finger on the straw, it will make a satisfying pop. This is like popping a balloon filled with air, although not as loud.

The sound from a popping straw can be loud enough to attract attention. Try to look innocent. Pretend that the straw exploded by itself.

("News flash: Straw explodes in restaurant. No injuries and no known causes. Story at 11:00.") If you draw the stares of the restaurant staff, plan on leaving a larger-than-normal tip.

An easy pickup

Can you pick up a bottle or can using only one straw?
At first it seems impossible. The trick is to bend the straw.

Start by bending the bottom inch of a straw
so the end touches the shaft of the straw.
Then lower the bend into an empty can
or bottle. Let the bent end open inside
the bottle or can, and pull it upward so
it catches on the underside of the can
top or in the neck of the bottle. Then
you can lift the container off the table.

Blow up your drink

Can you blow up your drink? Before
reaching for the dynamite, consider what
happens when you drink with a straw.
By sucking on the straw, you reduce the
air pressure in the straw, causing your
drink to rise. When you blow through the
straw, the opposite happens. You increase
the pressure in the straw and push the drink
downward. If you blow hard enough, you push all
the drink and some air out of the straw. You get bubbles.

But can you get soda to rise up the straw by blowing? Give it a try.
Hold the straw vertically in the beverage, and blow across the top.
You won't be able to watch while you are blowing, but your friends
will see the liquid rise. If you can't blow the drink up the straw, get
some bigger lungs working on the problem: Ask an adult to help.

To direct your lung power to the straw, you can make an aiming tube.
Starting about an inch from one end of a straw, cut three-fourths
of the way through it. Bend this top piece down to form a right angle
90 degrees). With the long end in your drink, you can blow through

the short piece. This aiming device will direct your breath across the top of the longer piece of the straw. See if this helps you blow the drink higher in your straw.

What's happening

By blowing across the straw, you reduce the pressure on the top of the straw. The faster air at the top pulls surrounding air along with it, and the air pressure is lowered. Meanwhile, the earth's atmosphere is pressing down on the beverage. Since you have lowered the pressure at the top of the straw and kept it the same at the bottom, fluid will rise. Your soda moves upwards.

If you were able to move some soda up the straw, you simulated a spraying device. One type of sprayer uses a garden hose hooked up to a container of fertilizer. The water flowing through the hose reduces pressure, draws up the liquid fertilizer, and shoots it out, along with the water. Speed indicators on airplanes use the same idea. As the plane flies faster, air moves faster across the top of a tube. This reduces the pressure in the tube and causes liquid in the tube to rise. By measuring the height of the liquid in a tube, the instrument measures the airplane's speed through the air.

While you are huffing and puffing on the straw, try sucking on two straws at the same time. Place one in your beverage and one outside the glass. Can you suck up some soda when one straw is sucking on air?

Siphons

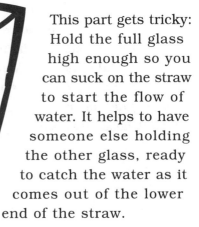

If your restaurant serves straws that bend, you can make a siphon. Take one glass that is filled to the top and another one that is empty. Bend the straw and place the short end in the full glass. Once you get the siphon working, you will want to put the longer end of the straw into the empty glass.

This part gets tricky: Hold the full glass high enough so you can suck on the straw to start the flow of water. It helps to have someone else holding the other glass, ready to catch the water as it comes out of the lower end of the straw.

As long as the full glass is higher than the receiving glass, the flow will continue.

With a flexible straw, you could raise one glass to get the drink flowing in one direction, and then raise the other glass to move the water back again. As long as the straw remains full, the siphon will operate and the flow will continue.

What's happening

Siphons work because there is more fluid on the lower side of the straw than on the higher side. The fluid flows down due to gravity. Because of the attraction between molecules of the drink, each molecule of the flowing liquid pulls along its neighbor.

If you cut even the tiniest of holes in the straw, however, the siphon fails. The drink will fall back down to both glasses.

Suck up soda

How much soda can you balance in the air with one finger? About a straw full. You can fill your straw with soda and keep it there by holding a finger over the upper end of the straw. Suck some drink up the straw. Quickly pull the straw out of your mouth, and slip a finger over the end. Now you can pull the other end of the straw out of the drink, and the liquid will stay captured in the straw. The stuff in the straw will stay there as long as you keep the top sealed. When you raise your finger off the straw, you will break the vacuum and release the drink. Try giving yourself a drink by lifting the filled straw above your mouth and then releasing your finger.

The empire straw building

Straws make great building materials. They are light, strong, and inexpensive. And, although you are limited in what you can build at a restaurant table, you can get a good start on a structure. The first problem to solve is getting a supply of straws. The second problem is to figure out how to connect straws.

There are several ways to attach one straw to another. The easiest way is to jam the end of one straw into the end of another. Other methods require paper clips, rubber bands, or adhesive tape. If you can find paper clips, you can bend open the clip and jam one curved end into one straw and the other end of the paper clip into a second straw.

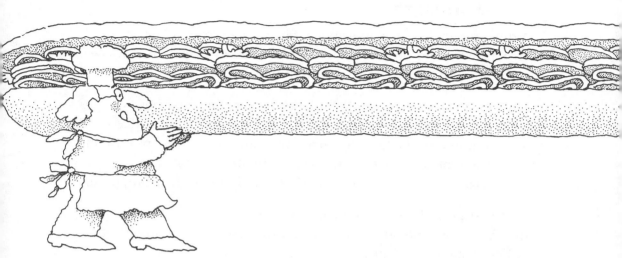

This allows you to connect two straws at any angle you want by bending the paper clip. Another type of connection requires rubber bands. You can connect two or more straws by wrapping their ends with a rubber band. Look around the restaurant to see what materials are be available. Maybe you'll get some inventive ideas of how to connect straws.

For your first construction project, make a triangle. Bend the straws to make the angles you need. If flexible straws are available, use the flexible part for the angles of the triangle. When you have made one, notice how strong it is. The triangle is a great shape to use in building structures because it distributes the weight along three sides and resists collapsing when pushed from the side. Try making a square with your straw and notice how easily it collapses when you press on the corners. Try the same thing with a triangle. You see triangles in bridge supports and buildings because triangles give strength.

If the restaurant is generous with the supply of straws, try building a small tower. Try different ways to stabilize the tower so it won't fall over. See if you can design your tower to use triangles.

Straw bridges

A different challenge is to see how far you can extend a straw structure beyond the edge of your table. You loose points, however, if restaurant staff or customers walk into it.

Start by anchoring one end of a straw under the sugar bowl or salt shaker. Then add a second straw extending over the floor. Keep adding straws until the weight of the structure causes it to collapse. No matter what material you use for a bridge, it can stretch only so far before its own weight exceeds its strength. That's why bridges have supports.

If your supply of straws is large, consider how you could strengthen the abyss-covering straw bridge. Can you make use of straw triangles to help hold it up? Can you reach the table closest to yours?

Straw tripods, billboards, & easels

Try making a tripod out of three or more straws. Once you have it erected, you can test its strength. Attach weights to the tripod to see how much it can hold. A paper clip would be handy here to help you attach things. Can your tripod support a wristwatch? A salt shaker? Several bags of sugar? Can you make a tripod strong enough to hold a paper napkin basket filled with pennies?

What sign should you put on top of the straw tripod? How should you identify your table? Maybe you could call your table the "Creative Corner," the "Idea Factory," or the "Wizard's Workshop." Do you want to proclaim this day to be a special occasion, someone's birthday for instance? Or would you like to impress the waiter to get faster service? You could put up a sign that identifies your table as a big-tipping table.

Since many restaurants favor having works of art (or at least pictures) hanging for your enjoyment, why not add to the decor with your own art? People at your table could draw some small pictures on their paper place mats, while others make easels out of straws to showcase the art. With a long wait for service, you could create an entire exhibit of art.

The last straw

With a straw, you can replicate an exhibit shown in many science museums. Museums use vacuum cleaners or large blowers to make a stream of wind that can support an inflated ball. You can try this with a straw.

This works exceptionally well with a straw and a ping-pong ball. However, if you neglected to bring a ping-pong ball with you to the restaurant, you might still be in luck. Try the ping-pong ball at home, but at the restaurant, be on the lookout for a pea.

Blow through the straw and hold the pea at the other end of the straw. With just the right amount of wind, you can get a pea to stay in the stream for a split second. Unfortunately, peas are not symmetrical, and they get tossed from the airstream. But keep searching for a perfectly round pea, and give your straw blower a try.

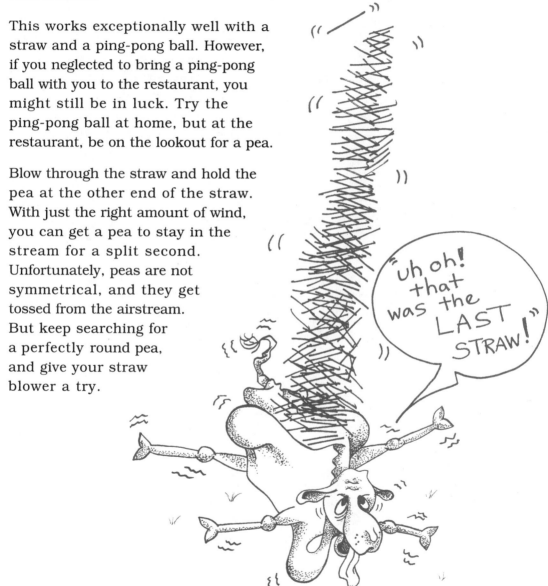

Really, this is the last straw. It's the straw that broke the camel's back. These phrases were coined by Charles Dickens in Dombey and Son. Dickens wrote: "As the last straw breaks the laden camel's back." Consider the implications. Since a robust camel can carry up to 1,200 pounds, and a straw weighs about 0.019 ounces, a camel could be carrying 1,011,526 straws before the last straw, number 1,011,527, would break its back.

2 Coffee chorus, tea tunes

An Ethiopian goat herder named Kaldi is credited with the discovery of coffee. He noticed that sheep stayed awake all night after eating the coffee plant. People used coffee as a medicine and a food before discovering its use as a beverage.

Hot designs

You can see interesting patterns on the surface of a very hot cup of coffee. Look at the coffee from different angles to get different lighting. Try to get the light to hit the coffee surface from the side, rather than from the top. Then you might see the irregular-shaped rings, or polygons.

What's happening

The rings are caused by the upward and downward flow of coffee. The hot coffee at the surface gives up heat to the cooler air above it. When it has given up heat, the surface coffee becomes cooler than the coffee below it. Since cooler liquids (generally) weigh more than hotter ones, the cooler coffee sinks. Warmer coffee from below rises to take its place at the surface. These upward- and downward-moving currents, called convection cells, make the patterns on the surface. The hotter liquid rises in the center of these cells, and the cooler liquid descends along the edges of the cells.

Instant coffee

If the restaurant serves instant coffee, make sure that you add the coffee to the hot water. Before you do, spin the hot water as fast as you can with a spoon. Then drop in a few granules of coffee. Try dropping them in the center of the cup and watch where they go. Then spin the water again and drop in a few more granules. This time place them closer to the edge of the cup. Do they move in the same direction?

Dropped near the edges, the granules of instant coffee fly to the outside and then move downward and dissolve. Dropped in the center of the vortex, they tend to stay there, spinning wildly until they dissolve.

Keep spinning and adding the instant coffee a little at a time. Finally, when the coffee is so black you can't see anything beyond the surface, it's time to add some cream.

25

Taking cream

Some fascinating things happen when you add cream to a cup of coffee. If you pour in just a little cream, watch as it mixes with the coffee. The cold cream falls to the bottom of the cup and then mixes upward until the black coffee turns brown. Whenever possible, ask for clear glass mugs so you can watch the patterns of cream.

If you are lucky enough to have a second coffee drinker who uses cream, stir the second cup before adding the cream. Get the coffee spinning really fast, but not so fast that it sloshes out of the cup. Notice that the surface of the coffee slopes downward toward the center of the cup. Then pour some cold cream into the center of the cup and watch the spinning cream descend to the bottom of the cup. Did the cream speed up or slow down the spinning?

This thought might keep you awake at night. Americans drink about 400 million cups of coffee every day.

You can repeat this experiment at home. You can use food coloring and hot water so you can see the flow in the cup. Another experiment to try is to pour in some corn syrup while the coffee (or just hot water) is spinning in a glass or cup. The dense syrup flows to the bottom and immediately slows the spinning liquid.

If people at your table are going to use dry cream, ask them to wait just a second. Before they put the creamer in their cups, tap the sides of the cups with a spoon. Notice the tone. Keep tapping lightly while they put the creamer in. The sound will change as soon as the creamer enters the coffee, and then it will revert back to the original tone.

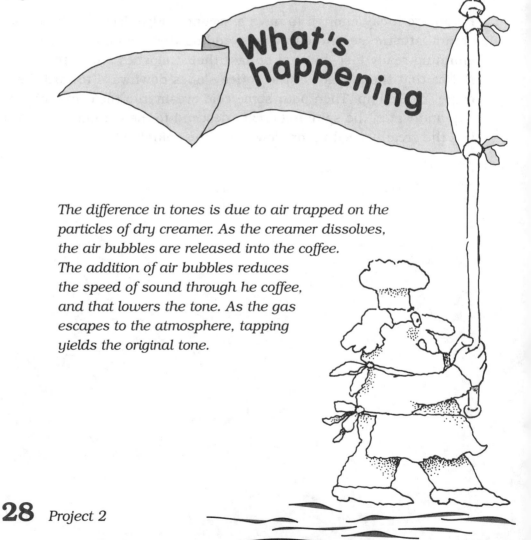

What's happening

The difference in tones is due to air trapped on the particles of dry creamer. As the creamer dissolves, the air bubbles are released into the coffee. The addition of air bubbles reduces the speed of sound through he coffee, and that lowers the tone. As the gas escapes to the atmosphere, tapping yields the original tone.

Cool it

Is the coffee too hot to drink? Try putting a spoon in the cup. The spoon will become warm quickly as heat moves from the coffee to the spoon. The spoon will conduct heat and radiate heat to the room. Having a spoon in the coffee will cool the coffee much faster than a cup without a spoon. You could try an experiment with two cups of coffee. Put a spoon in one, but not the other, and see which cools faster.

Feel the temperature of the spoon in hot coffee. That will convince you that the spoon is conducting heat from the coffee. Try a plastic spoon. Does it warm up as quickly as a metal spoon did? Which type of spoon would cool coffee faster?

To speed up the cooling, swirl the spoon in the coffee. This mixes the coffee, bringing the hotter coffee to the sides of the cup and to the surface where it can cool. Also try adding cream and sugar to see if you can detect a difference in the rate of cooling coffee with and without these additions.

Tea time *Tea was first used by the Chinese around the year 2740 B.C. Europeans were first exposed to tea in the early seventeenth century when Dutch traders brought it from Japan. American independence from England was partly brought about by resentment of the tax placed on tea imported from England into the colonies. The enraged colonists held the Boston Tea Party in 1773 to avoid paying the tax. The 100 colonists, dressed to look like Indians, dumped 342 chests of tea into Boston Harbor.*

Americans use about 3/4 pounds of tea per year per person. This compares to the 10 pounds of coffee that we consume.

TEA

Tea bags were invented by a man who wanted to send samples of tea to prospective customers. At the turn of the century, people bought tea in tin containers. It was impractical to send a tin of tea for someone to try, so Thomas Sullivan sewed tea bags out of silk. People liked the idea of having tea in self-contained bags, but the silk bags gave the brewed tea an unpleasant flavor. Several people tried to make tea bags out of other materials that would not impart a flavor.

One inventor, Faye Osborne, took up the challenge of making a better tea bag in the 1920s and continued working on tea bags until he retired in 1970. In 1942 he discovered a type of paper that was very thin, yet strong enough for tea bags. Two years later he found a way to heat-seal the bags shut, instead of sewing them shut. Today, about 95% of the tea sold in America is sold in tea bags.

For a change, order tea instead of coffee. Stir the tea and watch any loose tea leaves in the glass (ask for a glass cup instead of a ceramic one). The tea leaves accumulate in the center and swirl around, rising up toward the top and then falling back down again. By spinning the tea, you are creating a circulation pattern that has water rising in the center and falling along the outer edges. The tea leaves rise in the center with the circulating water. However, they usually settle back down to the bottom before reaching the top and swirling to the outer edge of the cup. As the spinning slows, the tea leaves settle on the bottom and spread out.

Iced tea was first served at the Louisiana Purchase Exposition in 1904. Richard Blechynden was the Englishman who created iced tea. His motivation was to increase sales of tea in the United States.

One pound of dried tea can make almost 300 cups of brewed tea.

3 It's in the bubbles

We owe the invention of soft drinks to Joseph Priestley. Priestley was unsuccessful as a preacher but more successful as a scientist. He conducted several experiments in a brewery. Noticing that there was a layer of gas (carbon dioxide) above beer, he tried to discover the nature of the gas. In one of his experiments, he found that he could capture gas bubbles in a glass of water. The bubbles gave the water a pleasant taste. Later, someone named the mixture soda water. Eventually the brewers threw Priestley out of the brewery when one of his experiments ruined a batch of beer.

Soda water became a popular drink in Europe. John Matthews invented a machine to inject carbonated gas into liquids in 1832. This made it much easier to make carbonated drinks and started people experimenting with adding flavors to soda water. By the late nineteenth century, a hundred years after Priestley made his discovery, soft drinks were being invented.

We called them soda, soft drinks, and pop. The name soda comes from Priestley's day, when carbonated water was called soda water. When flavors were added to soda water, the drinks were called soft drinks. The name soft drinks differentiated them from hard drinks, or drinks with alcohol. People enjoyed the bubbling of the soft drinks and started calling them soda pop, after the popping noise of the bubbles.

Coca-Cola was invented by a Georgia druggist, Dr. Julian Pemberton, in 1886. His mixture, still a trade secret and never patented, was made from coca leaves and cola nuts.

Many other drinks were created by druggists, but few of the early ones have survived. One early soft drink that has survived was named for a man who broke up a romance involving his daughter. The unsuccessful suitor was Wade Morrison. Many years after the failed romance, one of Morrison's employees created a new soft drink. In searching for a name for the drink, Morrison remembered his old romance and the man, Dr. Charles Pepper, who broke it up. He called his soft drink Dr. Pepper. Although he never won the hand of Dr. Pepper's daughter, Morrison did make his fortune using Dr. Pepper's name.

Clouds in your bottle

If your server brings you a sealed can or bottle of carbonated beverage, ask him or her not to open it. Gather your table companions around the can or bottle so everyone can watch closely as you open it. You can see two phenomena: bubbles being launched out of the container and a cloud forming in the opening of the container. The cloud can be difficult to see, and it is short-lived, so look closely.

What's happening

Bubbles form in the drink as carbon dioxide comes out of solution. These bubbles race to the surface and break. The explosion of bubbles sends droplets and other bubbles of drink into the air. You can catch some of the droplets and bubbles by holding a spoon beside the opening.

The salty feeling you get while sitting on an ocean beach results from a similar phenomenon. There, the crashing waves propel bubbles and droplets of salt water into the air. The water can evaporate, leaving particles of salt to be carried off by breezes. The salt particles attach to whatever or whomever they bump into.

What's happening

The cloud forms in a just-opened bottle because you released the pressure inside. In an unopened can or bottle, the pressure is about twice atmospheric pressure. Upon opening the drink, the pressure is released and drops to atmospheric pressure in the room. That reduction of pressure is enough to cause a drastic cooling of the gases in the container. The rapid cooling of the gases can cause a tiny cloud to form in the neck of the bottle. See if you can find a cloud in your bottle or can.

It's the bubbles

After you have checked out the cloud formation, pour your drink into a clear glass. It's fun to watch the bubbles form and rise to the surface. Bubbles form on tiny cracks in the glass and on any particles in the beverage.

Try placing a straw in the beverage and watching what happens as you raise and lower the straw. Bubbles of carbon dioxide will form on the straw. The motion of the straw will knock bubbles free, and they will rise to the surface. If you shake the straw vigorously enough, you will fill the end of the straw with a frothy mix of beverage and gas bubbles.

What's happening

The carbon dioxide in your drink comes out of the solution once you open the container. While the bottle or can is closed and under pressure, molecules of carbon dioxide are moving into and out of the solution (the drink). As long as the lid stays on, there is a balance between the number of molecules of carbon dioxide going from the drink into the gas in the container, and those going from the gas back into the drink. However, once the pressure is released upon opening, carbon dioxide bubbles come out of the solution, rise to the surface, and burst, releasing the carbon dioxide gas into the room.

If your carbonated beverage is in a clear glass, you can watch the bubbles form. Since bubbles tend to form in tiny cracks in the glass, see if you can find a site where bubbles are continuously being created.

Watch the bubbles form and rise. As a bubble falls upward, it enlarges and travels faster. The growth of bubbles is due to the decreased pressure encountered higher in the drink. As the bubble moves upward, there is less liquid above it, and thus lower pressure. As the pressure is reduced, the volume of the bubble increases.

Locate a site where bubbles are being released continuously. You will see that the spacing between bubbles increases as they rise in the drink. The bubbles are accelerating

upward, due to their buoyancy. As they speed up, they cover more distance, and the space between bubbles increases.

Bubble up

When you drop a straw into a carbonated beverage, you can watch the straw rise and fall by itself. As the carbonation (carbon dioxide gas)

comes out of the solution to form bubbles, some of the bubbles form on the sides of the straw. As more and more bubbles form, they give buoyancy to the straw and lift it. The bubbles act like hundreds of tiny life preservers, pushing the straw upward. As the straw rises, some of the bubbles break, and the straw falls back down. Eventually, as the drink warms up and the carbonation is expended, your drink tastes flat, and the straw stops rising and falling.

Bubble cascade

You can create an spectacular cascade of bubbles by supplying places for them to form. You can do the following experiment in either a soft drink or a beer. Although the experimental by-product of using a soft drink is all but undrinkable, using a clear one like 7-Up or Sprite provides good clarity, making the experiment easy to observe.

Shake some salt into the beverage. (Don't shake salt into someone's beverage unless the person has agreed to be part of this experiment). As grains of salt fall through the soda, gas bubbles form on them. The carbon dioxide dissolved in the soda comes out of the solution, where it encounters a grain of salt. The salt continues to fall through the soda, releasing bubbles, and the bubbles rise toward the surface. The total effect is a grand show. You will want to repeat it several times, eventually reducing the carbonation level to a point of "flatness."

Craig Bohren, in *Clouds in a Glass of Beer*, points out that salt in a beer is the analog of dust in the atmosphere. The salt gives carbon dioxide sites to form bubbles and come out of the solution. Dust particles in the atmosphere provide sites for condensation to occur. The dust helps clouds form. So peering into a salted beverage is analogous to doing research on cloud physics.

You might try other materials besides salt. Try sugar or pepper. See if they produce as voluminous a cascade of bubbles as salt does.

Fork frolics, spoon sports

In almost every restaurant, forks, spoons, and knives are provided. But it wasn't always so. Forks originated in Italy in the eleventh century, but they were a novelty and did not become popular. They even drew criticism from clergy, who thought that only people's fingers should touch food that was being eaten.

The French court used forks for the first time in 1589. Even with this official seal of approval, forks were not widely used for eating throughout Europe until the 1700s. As late as the end of the nineteenth century, the British Navy forbade use of forks and knives by sailors.

The earliest forks were two-pronged. French nobility adopted four-tined forks. Today, three-tined forks are the most common.

Forks are the most recent addition to the triad of utensils used today for eating. Knives were the first. They are among humanity's earliest inventions. Some scientists place their invention 1.5 million years ago. These ancient knives were made of flint. It wasn't until about 6000 B.C. that people started making knives of metal.

Spoons also found favor long before forks. Archaeologists have found spoons at relic campsites used 20,000 years ago. Spoons were made of wood and ivory, and much later, precious metals. Children of wealthy fifteenth-century parents were given silver spoons at the time of their baptism. This practice gave rise to the expression, "born with a silver spoon in her mouth."

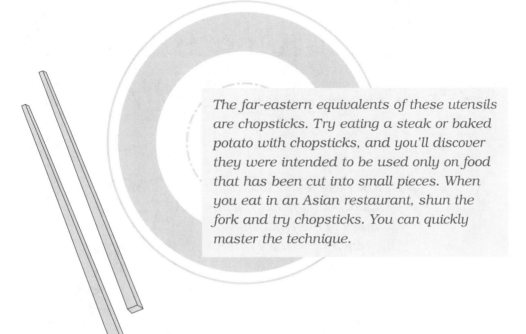

The far-eastern equivalents of these utensils are chopsticks. Try eating a steak or baked potato with chopsticks, and you'll discover they were intended to be used only on food that has been cut into small pieces. When you eat in an Asian restaurant, shun the fork and try chopsticks. You can quickly master the technique.

Balancing act

Try balancing two forks on the edge of a glass. Place a quarter between the tines of both forks to hold them together. Once you have the two forks firmly attached to each other, place the edge of the quarter on the rim of a glass. Orient the fork handles towards the glass. With a few tries, you can get the forks balanced.

It looks like it shouldn't balance, but it does. The handles of the forks shift the center of balance of the coin-forks structure so it is centered over the rim of the glass. Try balancing the coin and forks vertically on the bottom of an upturned (empty) glass or on your index finger.

Tuning forks

Forks make wonderful tones. Whack one against the table and listen carefully. Try holding the end of the fork on the table after you have hit the tines. Can you get the table to amplify the sound of the fork?

What's happening

Sounds are vibrations of air. By tapping the tines of the fork against the table, you start the tines vibrating. The vibrating tines vibrate the surrounding air, and you can hear the sounds. By placing the end of the fork against the table, you transfer the vibrations to the table to get its much larger surface vibrating. This concept of amplifying the sounds by transferring them to a larger surface or chamber is used in many musical instruments. The guitar is one example.

For even better sounds, support a fork with a piece of string. If you don't have string, a strip of paper napkin works as well. Tie the paper or string to the narrow part of the fork. Whack the tines with a knife, and listen to the melodious tones.

To get even better sounds, jam one end of the paper or string into your ear. Hold the paper there with one finger. Then whack the fork. The sounds are transmitted directly through the string or paper to your ear, so you hear them much better. You can hear the sounds even if the paper doesn't touch your ear. Try holding the paper on different spots on your head. The vibrations will be carried from the paper to the bones in your head, and you will hear sounds.

You can even feel the fork's vibrations in your teeth. Whack the fork on the table, and hold the handle between your teeth. If you had any doubts that the fork is vibrating, you won't doubt after it chatters your teeth. To avoid injuries, do not try to whack the fork while holding it in your teeth.

By now you have been whacking forks and sticking them all over your table and head. If all of this activity and noise hasn't attracted the attention of the other diners, you're in a really dull place.

Old spoon face

Can you get a spoon to stick to your nose? It is proper to try this, but only if you use your own spoon and your own nose.

Try holding a spoon on your nose. Unless you have a very unusual nose, the spoon won't stay put without some help.

You need to use some "glue." Exhale on the spoon to give it a layer of mist. Then press the spoon (the concave side, but you knew that) on your nose. With a little practice, you will amaze your friends and impress the waiters and waitresses. And, regardless of what they might say, it will look good on you.

Fun-house mirrors

Have you looked at yourself in the weirdly shaped mirrors at a carnival? You can appear tall and skinny or short and fat. See what reflections you can see with a spoon.

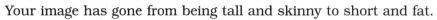

Hold the spoon up to catch your reflection in the bowl. Then flip the spoon over so the other side of the bowl faces you, and look again. On the concave side, you will appear upside down. On the convex side, you will be right-side up. Now rotate the spoon so the handle points sideways. Your image has gone from being tall and skinny to short and fat.

See what reflections you can get from your knife.

5 The *Maybe* splash zone: place mats

The hole-in-the-hand gang

You can make a hole appear in your hand by looking through a rolled-up place mat. Roll up a paper place mat into a tube, and hold it up to one eye so you can look through it, like a telescope. However, unlike using a telescope, keep both eyes open. If you are looking through the place mat tube with your right eye, hold the tube in your right

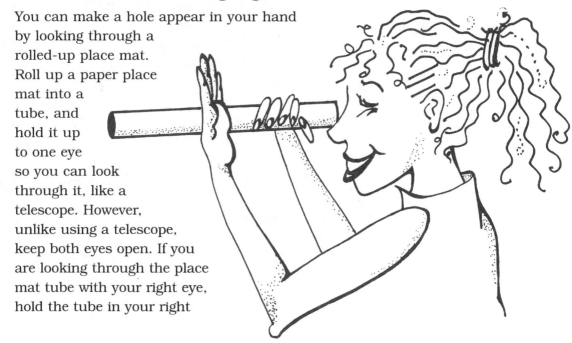

hand. Place your left palm next to, and perpendicular to, the tube. As you stare though the tube at the far end of the restaurant, you will see a hole in your left hand. If at first you don't see a hole, slide your left hand towards and away from you. With just a few seconds of experimentation, you will find the right placement.

Can you see the hole more easily if you use your other eye to sight in the tube? Give that a try. Then pass your tube around the table so everyone else can see the holes in their hands.

What's happening

Why does a hole appear in your hand? You see a hole because your left and right eye each view scenes from a slightly different perspective. One eye sees only the view through the tube and doesn't see your hand. The other eye sees your hand but not the view through the tube. Your brain has to make sense of the two different views and present you with one image, not two. The image it presents includes a hole in your hand.

In normal vision, your eyes see almost the same image, and your brain doesn't have to create an unusual image, like a hole in your hand. However, even in normal vision, the images are different. To see the difference, hold up your index finger at arm's length. Stare at your finger and at a reference point behind it. Now close one eye. Does the image jump? Open that eye and close the other one. You will find that closing one eye causes a much bigger change in the position of your finger relative to the background. The eye that causes the smaller change is your dominant eye. With both eyes open and viewing the same image, your brain tends to use the image of your dominant eye.

Tight squeeze

If you brought your Swiss army knife or a pair of scissors with you, try this trick. Trace the perimeter of a dime or a penny on your place mat, and cut a hole that size. Now try to squeeze a quarter through the hole, without ripping the paper. Can you do it?

You can push the quarter through if you fold the paper along one diameter of the hole. Try other coins to see which pairs work well.

If you haven't used up your supply of paper place mats, try this. Can you make a hole in your place mat big enough for you to step through it? Can you make a hole big enough to encircle the entire table? How can something as small as a place mat encircle something much bigger, like the table?

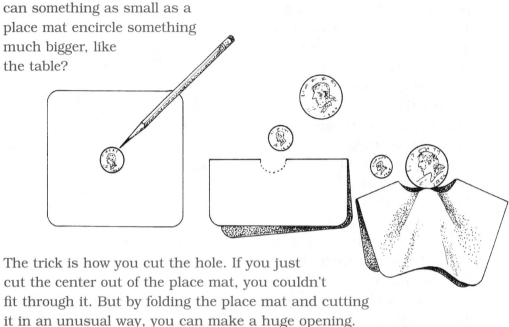

The trick is how you cut the hole. If you just cut the center out of the place mat, you couldn't fit through it. But by folding the place mat and cutting it in an unusual way, you can make a huge opening.

Fold the place mat in half. Cut or tear out a section 1 inch wide along the fold, leaving an inch along each end. Keep the place mat folded, and hold it with the folded side up. Starting at the inside edge of the section you removed, cut along a straight line toward the bottom edge, but leave an inch margin. Repeat this cut every ½ inch or so, ending at the other inside edge of the removed section. Turn the place mat around and, starting from the outer edges of the place mat, make cuts between each pair of the cuts you just made. Make sure you leave a ½-inch margin on the inside edge of these cuts.

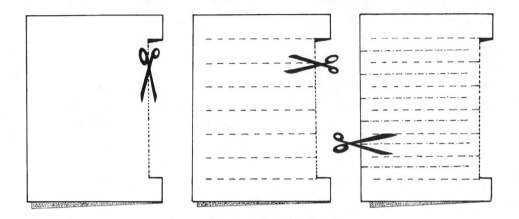

Now separate all the filaments of the place mat and open it up. Will it fit over you? With care, you could make more cuts in the paper to make a much larger hole. Give it a try.

Blow together

Here is a smaller-scale project requiring just two strips of paper torn or cut from a place mat. Cut the strips about 1 inch wide, across the width of the place mat. Dangle the two strips a couple of inches apart. What do you think will happen when you exhale between the strips? Will they move apart? Try it.

When you blew air between the strips, you reduced the air pressure there. The faster-moving air has lower air pressure, and the lower air pressure caused the strips to move towards one another. Try different separations of the strips and different air speeds.

Drawing stories

Blank place mats are empty canvases, waiting for your creative expression. If your place mat isn't blank, turn it over. With pencil, pen, or crayon make a picture story. Start by drawing an object, person, plant, or animal, and while you are drawing, tell a story about the picture. Then pass the place mat on to the next person. The challenge for the person is to add to your picture story by drawing and telling the next part. Let the story build as the place mat moves around the table. Everyone will have fun being wildly creative.

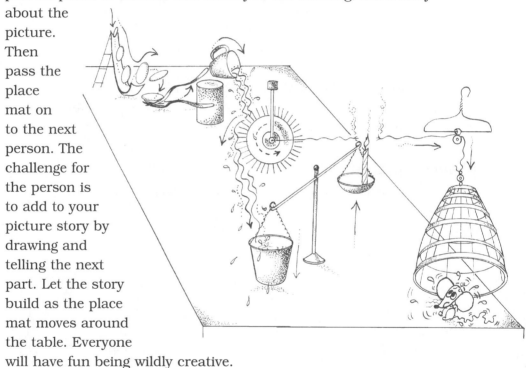

Or, instead of drawing a story, invent a better mousetrap. The goal is to get the mousetrap as complex as you can. One person starts by drawing one component of the mousetrap and explaining how it works. Then the next person adds one component to the design. The last person at the table has to complete the mousetrap by ensnaring the varmint.

Other place mat challenges include designing a flag that graphically represents who you are, or designing a space alien, a new restaurant, or cars from the twenty-first century. Or use the place mat to create your own cartoon comic strip.

6 Absorbing science: napkins

In ancient times, napkins were towel-sized pieces of cloth. Since people ate with their fingers, they needed a large cloth to clean them. When forks became popular, the need for large napkins diminished, and smaller napkins came into vogue.

Today, most
restaurants use
paper napkins, and
we will assume that
the napkins on your
table are paper.

Grease window

When you smudge a
greasy finger or two on
your napkin, look at
the grease spot. It
can appear either
lighter or darker
than the surrounding
paper, depending on
where the light is
coming from. When
you hold the napkin so light hits it from behind you, the grease spot
looks dark. The greasy paper is transmitting light through it, while

the nongreasy paper is reflecting more light back
to you. However, when you hold the napkin
up with a light behind it, the grease spot
looks lighter than the adjacent paper. It is
transmitting more light, while the
ungreased paper is reflecting it back,
away from your eyes.

See if the grease smudge transforms
the napkin from being translucent to
nearly transparent. Translucent
materials transmit light, but they
disorganize the light so you can't see

objects on the other side. When you hold the ungreased napkin up to a light, you can see light coming through it, but you can't see things on the other side. If you lay the napkin over the menu, you will find it difficult or impossible to read the entrees. But try reading through the grease spot. The grease spot lets light through and allows you to see things. It makes the paper transparent. Can you pick out a decadent dessert?

Wicked wick

You can make a wick out of a spare napkin. Roll up the napkin, or at least a strip torn from a napkin, and put one end in a glass of water. Put the other end in an empty glass. The water will be wicked up the napkin, soon soaking the entire napkin. Drops will fall into the empty glass. It will be a long time, however, before you have transferred much water. Hopefully, the service at your restaurant isn't so slow that the empty glass fills.

7 *Shake it out, spoon it on*

The phrase "not worth her salt" comes from the Medieval culinary practice of salting meat. If a piece of meat was so rancid that it would cost more in salt than the meat was worth, someone would say that the meat wasn't worth the salt. Salt then was much more expensive, relative to other commodities, than it is today.

Another version of the origin of this phrase is from Roman times. Roman soldiers received allowances to purchase salt (the origin of the word *salary*). A poor soldier wasn't worth his salt.

Making a map of your tongue

Your tongue has four types of taste buds, and each type is found on different parts of your tongue. Try this experiment. Pour a little salt on your index finger (you did wash your hands didn't you?) and place the salt on the tip of your tongue. Have a drink of water and repeat the test, but this time put the salt on the center of your tongue. Then try the sides of your tongue, and then try the back. Where is the taste strongest?

Now for the sweet stuff. Repeat the salt experiment with some sugar. Try pepper, too. You could draw a map of your tongue on a paper place mat. On your map, show where the sweet taste buds predominate and where the salt taste buds are located. Isn't it wonderful that the sweet taste buds are found up front? This lets you lick an ice cream cone to get the full flavor.

Salt cement

If your drink comes in a glass with ice cubes, you're in luck. Grab the ice cubes and set them on the place mat. If you lay one on top of another, not much happens, except they both melt. But if you spread some salt between two cubes and wait two minutes, you will find that the ice cubes fuse together. If you have trouble getting them to stick, squeeze them together for a few seconds.

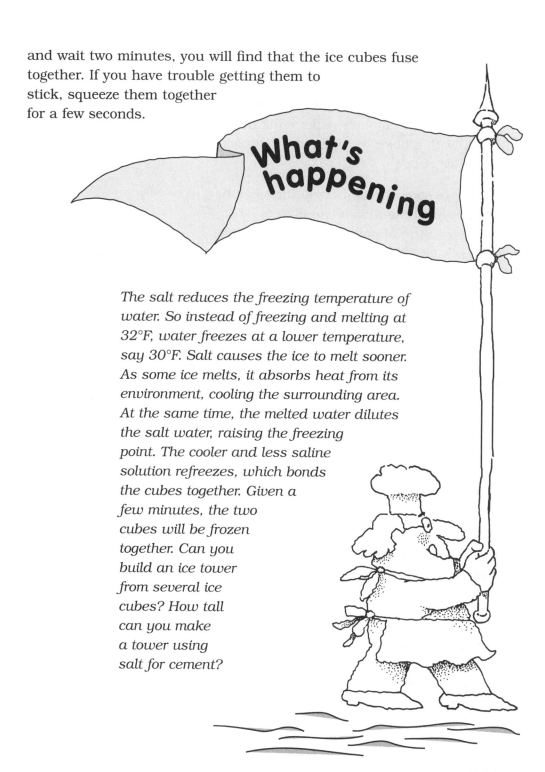

What's happening

The salt reduces the freezing temperature of water. So instead of freezing and melting at 32°F, water freezes at a lower temperature, say 30°F. Salt causes the ice to melt sooner. As some ice melts, it absorbs heat from its environment, cooling the surrounding area. At the same time, the melted water dilutes the salt water, raising the freezing point. The cooler and less saline solution refreezes, which bonds the cubes together. Given a few minutes, the two cubes will be frozen together. Can you build an ice tower from several ice cubes? How tall can you make a tower using salt for cement?

An easy pickup

You can do a fun trick with salt and ice. But you also need a piece of paper. Rip a strip of paper from your paper napkin. Now, armed with a piece of paper, can you pick up an ice cube?

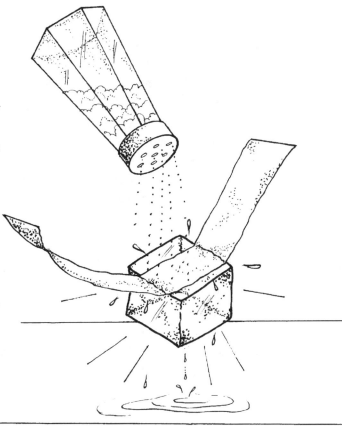

Challenge someone to pick up the ice cube without touching it. You can do this by laying the strip of paper on the cube of ice, then salting it. The salt will speed the melting and refreezing of the ice.

You can try this with a thread; however, it is more difficult to do. No thread? Pull a pocket inside out. Undoubtedly you will find a thread there. If not, look inside your coat or along the cuff of your pants. With your ever-handy pocket knife, cut off a few strands and repeat the experiment using thread instead of paper.

Try these experiments again, replacing the salt with sugar. Does it work as well? Why do we use salt instead of sugar on highways in winter?

Salt crevasses

With one or two ice cubes in the bottom of a glass or on a plate, pour on a little salt. In a few minutes, you will see crevasses form in the ice as the salt appears to eat its way through the ice. Salt lowers the freezing point of water to below 32°F. Since the cube is at (or near) 32°F, the area around each grain of salt melts. The grains can melt their way through an ice cube, and the melted water can cool and refreeze above the salt.

Is someone at your table the "salt of the earth?" The phrase was used in biblical times. The earliest written use of it occurs in the book of Matthew, where Jesus called peacemakers, those pure of heart, and the meek the salt of the earth and the light of the world.

Totally electric

You can pick up salt or pepper with a comb. It is even easier to do with a balloon instead of a comb. But to get a balloon, you have to be at one of the best restaurants, the ones that give out balloons. Get a good static charge on your comb or balloon. Rub the comb through your hair, or rub the balloon on your shirt or coat. Rubbing a balloon on carpet also works well, if you don't mind crawling on your hands and knees in a public restaurant.

While you are getting a charge, have one of your dinner companions spread some salt or pepper on a place mat. Or mix the two ingredients together. Bring your electrically charged wand (comb or balloon) to the pile and watch grains jump up and stick to the balloon or comb. If you slowly lower the charged wand over a pile of salt and pepper, you can pick up the pepper, but not the heavier salt. As you lower it farther, even the salt will jump up. Try picking up tiny scraps of napkin with your charged comb or balloon.

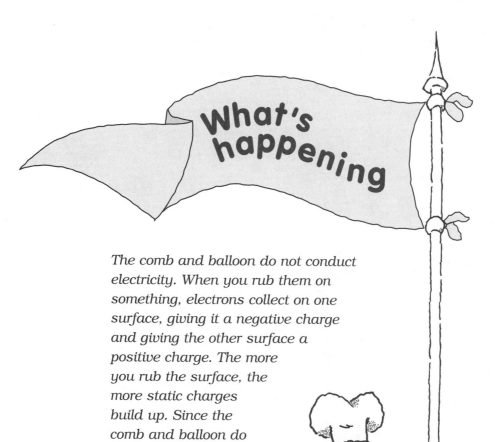

What's happening

The comb and balloon do not conduct electricity. When you rub them on something, electrons collect on one surface, giving it a negative charge and giving the other surface a positive charge. The more you rub the surface, the more static charges build up. Since the comb and balloon do not conduct electricity, the charge tends to stay there until it is neutralized by attracting oppositely charged particles.

8 *Galloping glasses*

Puzzle to ponder

Before your glasses are filled, try this game. Set two glasses upside down, and put one glass between them right-side up. The game is to take exactly three moves, inverting two glasses each move, to get them all right-side up. If you start by inverting the center glass and one outside glass, and then the two outside glasses, on your third move you will put all three right-side up.

In this game you have three turns to move two glasses each turn. That's a total of six flips. With one glass upright (and two down), you use two flips to move that glass upside down and then right-side up. You flip one of the end glasses just once to get it upright. That leaves three flips (of the total of six flips) to use on the other outside glass, which leaves it upright.

What's happening

Starting with two glasses right-side up requires an odd number of flips to get all of them right-side up. For example, you could get them all right-side up by flipping the center glass just once. Since the rules require you to use an even number of flips (six), you can't solve the puzzle when you start with one glass down and two up.

Now challenge someone else to repeat what you just did. Only this time start with the center glass up and the outer glasses down. It seems that this should be just as easy, but it's not. If you slyly turn over the center glass after performing the trick the first time, you can fool an unsuspecting dinner companion into undertaking an impossible challenge.

Now hear this

Try holding up a glass to your ear. We suggest you use an empty glass, but you could be more daring. Can you hear the ocean? If you started with a full glass, wait until the tide ebbs, then listen for the ocean. What is that sound?

The glass, like a seashell, vibrates at its natural frequency. It picks up sound energy—from the conversations at the next table, the waiter shuffling past, and blood circulating in your ear—and transfers that energy to sounds at its natural frequency or tone. Frequencies close to the natural frequency of the glass are favored and are the ones you hear.

Once you have marveled at the sounds inside your glass (and people at nearby tables have figured out that you have lost your marbles), try glasses of other sizes. Big ones give deep tones, and fine wine glasses give higher pitches. Of course, if your table has fine wine glasses on it, you might refrain from this exercise, at least until no one is looking.

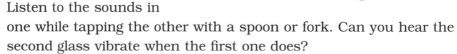

Identical glasses have the same natural frequency of vibration, and if you vibrate one it will excite its identical neighbor. Place two identical glasses near each other on the table. Listen to the sounds in one while tapping the other with a spoon or fork. Can you hear the second glass vibrate when the first one does?

Bays on the coast have natural frequencies, just like glasses do. Their vibrations are much slower and can be seen in the movement of water instead of being heard. Those bays with natural frequencies close to the tidal frequencies can have huge tides, like the Bay of Fundy in Nova Scotia. Nearby bays that have different sizes and shapes, and hence different natural frequencies, have much lower tidal ranges.

Can you see it?

Your water glass makes a great lens. You can see much better if there is no ice in the glass. Take a paper place mat and draw a large arrow on it pointing to one side. Hold the arrow behind the glass and look at it through your glass from across the table. As the arrow moves behind the lens, it changes direction. Magic? No, the water bends light waves just like a magnifying glass and your eyes do. Try holding the arrow at different distances from the glass. Can you use the glass to magnify things? Can you use it to read the fine print on the menu?

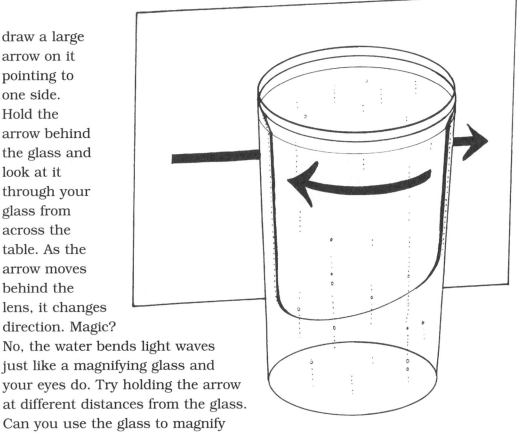

Milk residue

When you are drinking milk, do you ever look at the bottom of the glass? Check it out. Hold the glass at an angle so that milk covers about half of the bottom of the glass. You will see a film covering the upper half of the bottom, with the milk covering the lower half. But, just between them, you can find a clean line separating the two. No one knows why this line appears, so enjoy the mystery of milk residue.

If anyone asks what you are doing staring in the bottom of a glass of milk, tell them you have found a way to read the milk, like tea leaves. Tell them you will read their fortune, for a small fee. They are more likely to believe you than if you tell them you are doing a science experiment. And maybe you can pick up some pocket change.

Glass tunes

Something that is always fun to do with glasses is to try to play a tune with them. If you have several glasses, you can set them up with different levels of water in each. Tap them lightly with a spoon or knife to make pleasant tones. Can you adjust the level of water to give each glass a musical note?

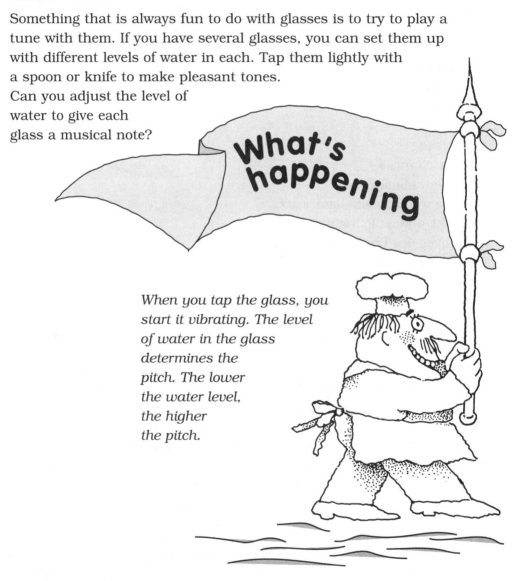

What's happening

When you tap the glass, you start it vibrating. The level of water in the glass determines the pitch. The lower the water level, the higher the pitch.

Try rubbing the top of a glass with a moistened finger. Hold the base of the glass tightly to the table. With a thin glass and just the right amount of moisture on your finger, you can get the glass to sing. Try several glasses with different levels of water. Experts can play music on glasses.

What's happening

When you rub your finger across the glass, you are vibrating the glass and the water in it. Your finger slides along the rim, then sticks, then slides again. These starts and stops cause the glass to vibrate. The vibrations cause sounds. A creaking door makes sounds the same way, as the hinge slips and sticks while opening.

Size up your glass

Look at the glasses on the table. Which do you think is larger, the height of each glass or its circumference? How could you tell?

Try measuring a glass. You could use a strip torn from your paper napkin for a measuring tape. Wrap the strip around the rim of your glass and mark it with a pencil or a small tear to record the circumference. Then hold the measured strip next to your glass. You might be surprised to see that the circumference is larger than the height. Except for the skinniest and tallest glasses, the rim is always longer than the glass is tall.

9 Kindling candles

A blowout

It's fun to have candles on your table. Just watching them burn is fun. Try blowing gently on a candle. As you blow, the flame moves away from you, downstream. Now do the same thing, but hold your knife 2 inches in front of the flame. Now when you blow, the flame will lean towards you. If you don't get this to happen, move your knife towards or away from the candle until you get the flame leaning towards you.

In each case the flame moves downstream in the stream of air. In the first case, it is obvious which direction is downstream; it's the direction you are blowing. In the second case, however, blowing on your knife creates an eddy. As air moves around the knife, it curls back towards the center and moves back towards you. The flame is pulled along by the flow of air.

If you blow out the candle (make sure that you have cupped a hand behind it to prevent hot wax from being blown across the table), the candle smokes for several seconds. The smoke is the product of incomplete combustion. The three things needed for fire—heat, fuel, and oxygen—are all present, and combustion continues. However, without the flame, there isn't enough heat to burn the fuel completely. The incomplete combustion leaves lots of residue that rises as smoke.

When you watch a movie of a steam locomotive, you can tell when the engineer has the fire adjusted correctly. If lots of dark smoke is pouring out of the stack, combustion is incomplete, probably due to a lack of oxygen. When properly adjusted, smoke comes out white or with little color at all.

How does a candle produce light? Light is produced when electrons are excited by receiving energy and then return to their normal energy levels. When they return, they give off photons of light. For candles, the energy source that excites the electrons is the heat of combustion.

What is burning in the candle? The wick is burning at an exceptionally slow pace, so it can't account for all of the heat. The solid candle isn't burning. If it could burn, wouldn't it catch on fire when the wick was lit? Obviously the flame itself is important since the candle doesn't give off light until it is lit.

The flame melts the candle, creating a pool of liquid wax. The wick draws this liquid up towards the flame, where the liquid is vaporized. The vapors mix with air (rich with oxygen) and ignite. The heat released from the combustion provides the energy to excite the electrons in the wax vapor. When the electrons return to their normal, lower energy levels, they emit photons of light. That's a lot of stuff happening just because you wanted to play with a candle!

To extinguish the flame, all you need to do is remove one of the three essential ingredients of fire: combustible material, heat, or oxygen. When you moisten your fingers and grab the wick, you are cooling it below the point of combustion. You can also remove all of the oxygen to extinguish the flame. Many types of fire extinguishers take this approach; they spread carbon dioxide, which, being heavier than air, pushes away the air and its oxygen.

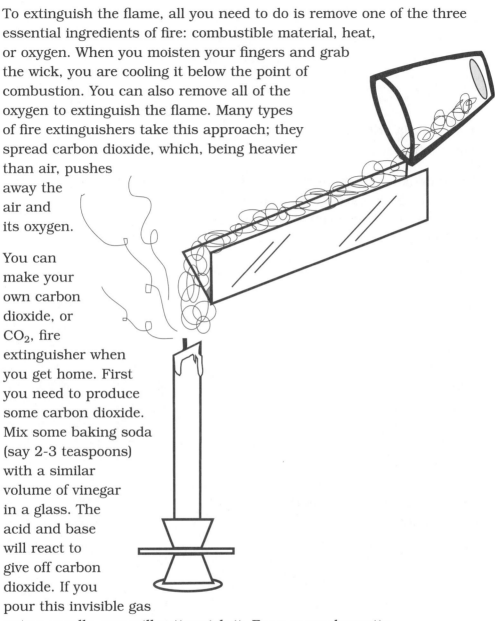

You can make your own carbon dioxide, or CO_2, fire extinguisher when you get home. First you need to produce some carbon dioxide. Mix some baking soda (say 2-3 teaspoons) with a similar volume of vinegar in a glass. The acid and base will react to give off carbon dioxide. If you pour this invisible gas onto a candle, you will extinguish it. For a more dramatic demonstration, make a trough out of aluminum foil and pour the relatively heavy gas into the trough. It will flow down the trough to the candle, putting it out.

Sitting at a restaurant, you probably don't have a box of Arm & Hammer Baking Soda and a bottle of vinegar. But you can get some CO_2 from your soda. Since carbon dioxide is in solution in your soda or beer, you just have to figure out how to release and capture the gas.

To extinguish a burning candle with the carbon dioxide from your soda, it helps to have a small candle. How small? It should be so small that it will fit inside your glass. That's the size of a candle from a birthday cake.

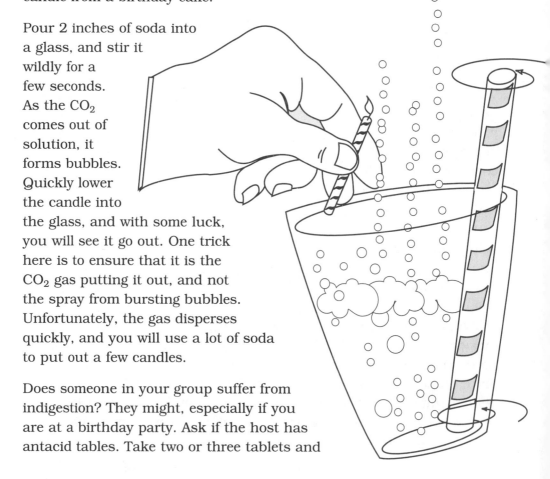

Pour 2 inches of soda into a glass, and stir it wildly for a few seconds. As the CO_2 comes out of solution, it forms bubbles. Quickly lower the candle into the glass, and with some luck, you will see it go out. One trick here is to ensure that it is the CO_2 gas putting it out, and not the spray from bursting bubbles. Unfortunately, the gas disperses quickly, and you will use a lot of soda to put out a few candles.

Does someone in your group suffer from indigestion? They might, especially if you are at a birthday party. Ask if the host has antacid tables. Take two or three tablets and crush them into a fine powder in a dry glass. You can use Rolaids or Tums, but not Tagamet. Tamaget isn't an antacid medicine; it is a medicine to prevent acid from being secreted in your stomach.

What can you use for an acid? At home you can use vinegar. At the restaurant, use some of your soda. You can pour the soda into the glass with the ground-up antacid tablets to get a rapid bubbling of CO_2. Some of the gas is liberated by having the fine powder in the soda, just as salt grains would free the gas. And some of the gas is liberated from the reaction of an acid (your soda) with a base (the antacid tablets). Lower a birthday cake candle into the glass to see it extinguished by the CO_2. (Be careful with the flame, and ask an adult to supervise you.) By the way, the grinding up of the tablets allows them to be dissolved much more quickly, which produces the gas quickly. If you don't grind them up, the production of carbon dioxide is so slow that you won't be able to put out even a tiny candle.

Another way to extinguish a flame is to pump air onto it. Take an empty soda can (are you sure it is empty?) and hold it an inch away from a candle. Then squeeze the can as hard as you can. As you crush the can, you will create a gust of wind strong enough to extinguish the flame.

Admittedly, it would be easier just to blow the candle out. But what's the fun of that?

10 It's a stick-up

Friction matches, Teflon, Ivory Soap, ScotchGuard, and microwave cooking all have one thing in common. All of these were discovered by accident. The invention of friction matches occurred during experiments on explosives. In 1826, John Walker was trying to find new explosives. When he scraped some experimental residue off of a wooden stick, it burst into flames. Walker did not patent his discovery, but others did pursue commercial success with his invention. One result of the introduction of an easy-to-use match was a dramatic increase in the number of people smoking tobacco.

Many people made improvements to the match. One major advancement was the invention of the safety match. A German chemistry professor came up with the idea of putting one part of the combustible materials on the match head, and the other parts on a striking surface on the matchbox. Having the two necessary components separated lessened the likelihood of an accidental ignition.

Diamond Match Company designed the style of matchbook that is used today. The company placed matches inside a book and put the striking surface on the outside cover of the book. Once Diamond invented the matchbook in 1895, it took less than a year for a brewer to start an advertising trend by printing an ad on the cover.

Pick 'em up

You can create your own version of the game in which you try to force your opponent to pick up the last match. Lay out some number of matches (or substitute toothpicks) in pairs. Five pairs is a good number to start. Each person picks up at least one match, but not more than three matches during each turn.

After you play a few games, you will catch onto the strategy that lets you win every game. Then you can change the number of matches you lay down, the number you pick up, or the objective of the game. For example, you could change the goal of the game to pick up the last match.

Inventing these games is as much fun as playing them. So you can create a new game every time you dine out.

Match this

This is a hokey trick. Challenge someone to predict which side of a cardboard match will land face up when you toss it into the air. Point out that the match has four sides; two sides are wide, and two edges are quite narrow. Your friend can choose any two of the four sides. Of course, the savvy opponent will choose the two wide sides. To ensure that there is no confusion on which sides your friend chose, you can mark both of his or her choices with  a pen. You take the remaining sides (edges) that don't have marks on them. By now, your friend is convinced that you have lost all of your mental matches.

However, you do have a trick. Just before you toss the match in the air, give it a sharp bend in the middle. If you bend it quickly, your friend won't see you do it. However, your friend will notice that the match is bent when he or she sees it lying on the table. Your friend will notice that because he or she will be surprised to see the match lying on one edge. A bent match will almost always land on its edge. If it lands on one side, it will be unstable, and even the smallest vibration will cause it to land on its edge. Just give it a try.

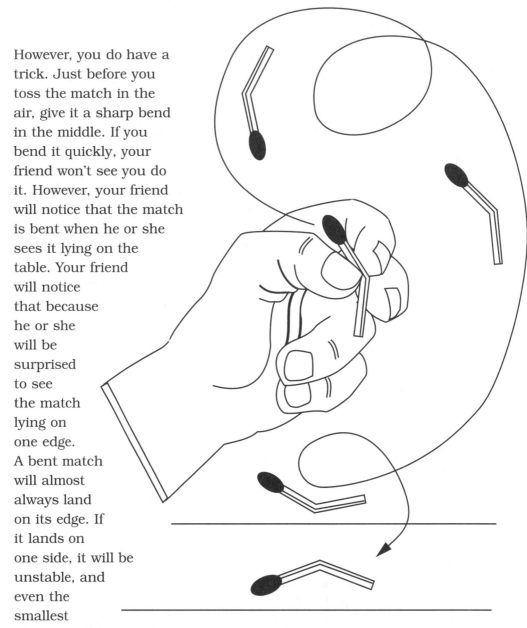

Matchbox magic

As long as you are playing games on your table partners, try this one. See if your restaurant offers matches in boxes. If you can find a box, challenge someone to drop the box onto the table so it ends up standing on one end. Several attempts will convince the person that the task is impossible; the box will fall over every time

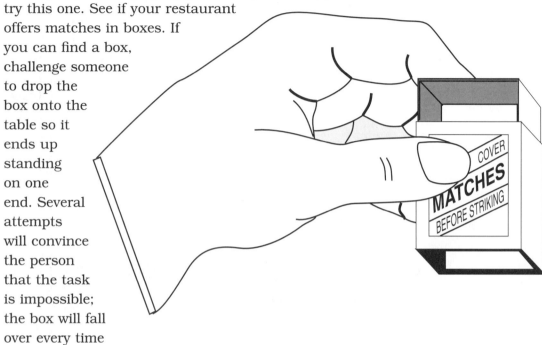

after it lands on the table. However, you can do this stunt.

When it is your turn to demonstrate, push the drawer containing the matches out of the box by an inch or so. The drawer should be

sticking up towards the ceiling when you drop the box. Hold the box about 3 inches above the table. When the box hits the table, the drawer will shut and the box will remain upright.

What's happening

With the drawer closed, the box bounces off the table and lands on its side. With the drawer open, the box slides toward the table upon impact, absorbing energy more gradually and standing upright.

Finally, a use for peas

What do you do with a plate full of peas—especially if they recently came out of a tin can? The best thing to do with them is press them into service to create a pea tower.

Grab a fistful of toothpicks and begin building your tower. The utilitarian peas allow you to connect two or more toothpicks. Just stab the green balls and implant the toothpicks.

Try making triangles and squares to use in structures. When your tower rises above the centerpiece on your table and you have run out of peas, ask your fellow diners for their unwanted peas. They will gladly donate to such a worthy cause.

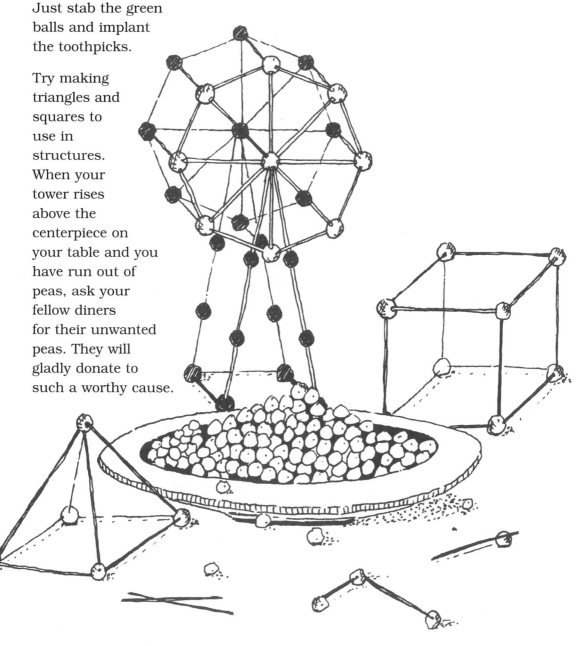

Pocket change

Change is good. So try to get some. Take a collection of coins at your table. For that matter, take a collection at the next table, too. Tell them you are conducting an important test on the U.S. coinage system.

Once you have a big stack of coins, check them out. The phrase "E Pluribus Unum" appears on every U.S. coin. It means "out of many, one," and it

refers to the thirteen colonies coming together to form one country.

Locate the date on each coin and look for a mint mark near it. Coins minted in Philadelphia are marked with a "P." The other large mint, in San Francisco, stamps an "S" on some of the coins produced there. There are two smaller mints: at Denver (mint mark "D") and at West Point (mint mark "W"). However, you will notice that many coins don't have any mark. Did the mint run out of letters, or weren't they proud enough of this batch to put their mark on them?

You can also find the phrase, "In God We Trust." This phrase was added to U.S. coins starting in 1864.

Have you noticed that dimes, quarters, half dollars, and silver dollars have milled edges? Pennies and nickels have raised edges instead of milled edges. Milling the edges of coins became necessary (in the sixteenth century) when people starting chiseling off the edges of coins. This is the origin of the term "chiseler" to denote a person who cheats. Chiselers would knock off a piece of the precious metal coin with a hammer and chisel. Then they would spend the coins. Since all coins had irregular edges, no one would

The first coins were minted around 600 B.C. in western Turkey. However, 500 years before that, the Chinese were using miniature replicas of bronze tools for currency.

notice that a coin had been chiseled. (The only way to know that a coin had the official weight of gold or silver was to weigh it. Imagine having to carry a scale in your pocket or backpack). When the chiselers had collected enough chips of gold or silver, they could sell the metal. When this practice became widespread, governments had to invent something to stop it. That something was the milled edge. So every time you feel the milled edge of a coin, think of the chiselers.

Temple rubbing

You can copy the pattern from a coin onto your paper place mat. The technique is the same one used to replicate the patterns found in the architecture of ancient temples.

Lay your place mat over a coin. Using the side of a pencil lead, rub it over the place mat covering the coin. With just a few strokes, you will see the outline of the coin. Sometimes, if the pattern on a coin has been worn

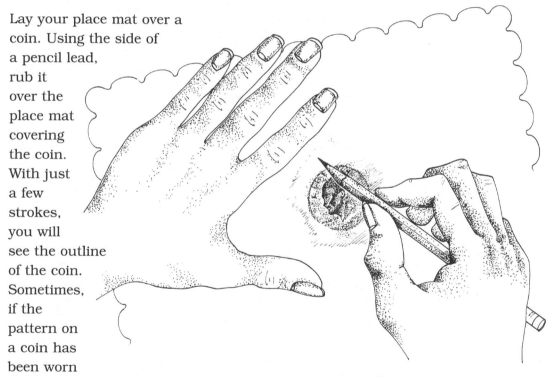

away, the pattern is easier to see by looking at the rubbing instead of the coin itself. If you don't have a pencil, try a pen. Crayons work great, too. Ask the server if your restaurant has some.

What's happening

As you press on your pencil or pen, it leaves marks on the paper where it is supported by the raised images on the coin. Your pencil tends not to leave a mark where the paper is unsupported, thus giving you an image of the coin.

Making a third coin appear

If you hold two coins between your index fingers and rub them together, you can make a third coin appear. You won't be creating a new coin, but you will see one. Move the two coins back and forth as quickly as you can. The third coin should appear between and under the two other coins.

What's happening

You see the third coin because the coins are spinning too fast for your brain. Your brain can handle at most about 10 images per second. When you bombard it with more images than that, it can make up a story of what it thinks it sees. In this case, you see another coin. In other situations, your brain can make you think you are seeing moving images when you are seeing still images.

Movie projection systems flip at least 24 frames (of still images) per second in front of your eyes. But you don't see the individual still images. Instead, you see continuous movement. Thomas Edison, who invented the movie projector, did some of the earliest research to determine how many images he had to project each second to fool the brain.

Movies flicker images 24 times per second, and television screens flicker images at the rate of 30 times per second.

Just as your eyes were fooled by the moving coins, the camera is fooled when it views something that moves too quickly for it to record. If you watch old western movies, you might see the wagon wheels appear to move backwards while the wagon is moving forwards. In this case the spokes are moving faster than the camera is recording images. To provide more realistic images of motion, advanced entertainment systems use even higher rates of speed than 24 or 30 images per second.

Making change

You can take the bottom coin from a stack of coins without upsetting the rest of the stack. An easy way to do this is to build a stack of quarters on top of a penny. Then lay a dime next to the stack. Flick the dime with your forefinger so it whacks the penny and knocks it out from under the stack. With some practice, you can replace the penny with the dime under the stack. Try other combinations of coins to see which coins you can replace.

What's happening

This experiment demonstrates inertia. The stack of quarters stays at rest. If you hit the penny underneath the stack hard enough, it will slip out from under the stack. At the collision, the momentum of the dime will be transferred to the penny, and the quarters will stay put.

A second demonstration of inertia requires a strip of your paper place mat. Lay the end of the strip on an empty glass. Balance two quarters on top of the strip, on the edge of the glass. Now can you withdraw the strip without causing the quarters to fall?

If you tug gently on the paper strip, you will pull the quarters off their perch. To get them to stay there, you have to remove the paper quickly. The easiest way to do that is by holding the end of the paper and hitting the middle. Grab the end and hold it nearly taut. Then, being careful that you won't hit something on the table, hit the middle of the strip with your hand. To get this to work, you have to move your hand as fast as you can. If the coins fall when you try this, add a couple of more coins to the pile. The more coins there are, the more inertia there will be and the more likely it will be that the stack will remain on the edge. Also, it might be a good idea to have someone hold the base of the glass so it doesn't get upset.

Coins in a fountain

Well, even if you can't have coins in a fountain in the restaurant, you can have coins in your glass. If you have a glass of water without ice, try dropping a coin in your glass. Before you let go, predict how it will fall in the glass. If you let it fall with one edge pointing downward, will it hit the bottom of the glass in that position? Will it fall differently if you release it with a flat side parallel to the water's surface? Give it a try. You might be surprised at how coins tumble.

Until recently coins had an intrinsic value. A silver dollar had a dollar's worth of silver. Now coins are made of metals of lesser value. If you melted a nickel, you wouldn't get 5 cents worth of metal. In fact, if you melted a nickel, you would find that it was made of a combination of copper and nickel. The coins with milled edges (dimes, quarters, and half and silver dollars) are sandwiches of a copper core covered with a copper-nickel alloy.

Now that you have a coin in the bottom of the glass, what do you do? See if you can see an image of the coin on the surface of the water. Begin your search by looking with your eyes level with the water's surface. Then move them upward. If you don't see the image, take a drink out of your glass to lower the water level, and try again.

If you can find the image, you can make it disappear merely by placing your hand behind the glass. If that doesn't make the image go away, moisten your hand and grip the glass with it. Now you can make the image appear and disappear by moving your hand. Why does the placement of your hand affect the image of coin?

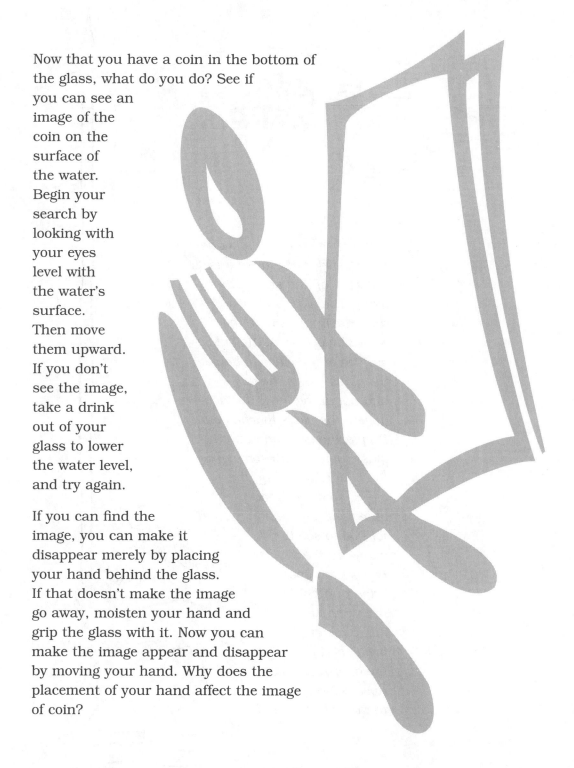

What's happening

You can see the coin's image
on the surface because it is
reflected off the side of the
glass. The glass acts like
a mirror. In particular, the
reflection occurs at the outer
surface of the glass (where
the glass meets the air)
and not at the inner surface
(where the glass touches water).
By placing your hand on the
glass, you absorb some of
the light reflected off the
glass, so there is too
little light remaining
for you to see the
image on the surface.
By wetting your
hand and holding
the glass, you
make better
contact with
the glass and
absorb more
of the reflected light.

Erupting dime

If someone ordered a beverage that came in a bottle, ask the person if you can use the empty bottle. Tell the person you want to start an eruption.

Moisten the lip of the bottle and place a dime on it. Then grasp the bottle with both hands and hold it for a few minutes. Be careful to hold the bottle flat on the table so you don't knock off the dime accidentally.

As your hands warm the air inside the bottle, air pressure will rise and try to escape. The only way for it to vent is by moving the dime. The dime will dance up and down. Could you make a dime erupt using a bottle filled with a beverage? If you're not sure, give it a try. Happy eruptions.

Spinners and sliders

You can make up some great games with two or three coins and a smooth tabletop. One game is to see who can roll a coin off the far side of the table. Hold the coin on edge with one forefinger and spin the coin with a flick from your other forefinger. While it is spinning, catch it on its edge with one finger. It might take some practice to be able to catch the coin like this, but you will master the technique in a few minutes.

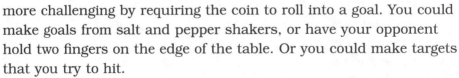

Once you can catch the coin on its edge, roll it towards the "end zone," your partner's side of the table. When this becomes too easy for you, make the game more challenging by requiring the coin to roll into a goal. You could make goals from salt and pepper shakers, or have your opponent hold two fingers on the edge of the table. Or you could make targets that you try to hit.

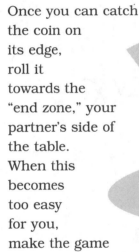

Another coin game is Sliders. The goal of Sliders is to slide a coin as close to the edge as you can without causing the coin to fall off the table. If you slide the coin over the edge, you lose that inning. After the first person slides, the person sitting opposite the first

player takes a turn. The person who slid his or her coin closest to the edge (without going over) wins the inning.

You can make soccer goals, hockey goals, or a basketball hoop with your hands. Slide coins or fling them with opposing thumbs into your opponent's goal. Or invent your own game. Coming up with a game is as much fun as playing. So have fun.

Blow some money tonight

Can you blow a dime into a glass or cup? It might sound impossible, but you can do it. Place a dime on the table, one dime's diameter from the edge. Hold the tilted edge of a cup or short glass about two dimes' diameters farther from the dime. If you give a sudden and hard blast of breath, you can get the dime to jump into the cup.

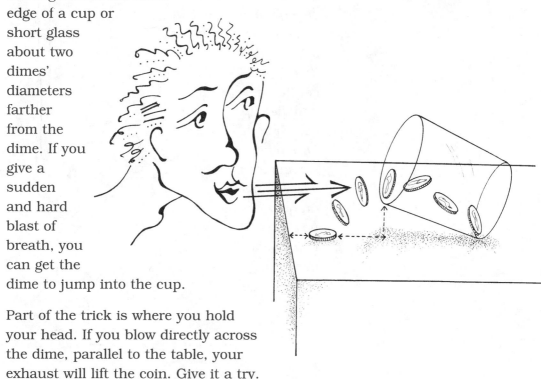

Part of the trick is where you hold your head. If you blow directly across the dime, parallel to the table, your exhaust will lift the coin. Give it a try.

What's happening

Fast-moving air has lower pressure, so your blast of air reduces the air pressure above the dime. The pressure is reduced enough to lift the dime. Other coins are harder to lift, but give them a try. To get the dime into the cup, your breath had to be moving at least 30 miles an hour. And you thought you couldn't move that fast?

12 Dessert trivia

Appetizers

On average, humans eat about 1,000 pounds of food a year. Here are some bites of trivia on the 1,000 pounds you ate last year.

In the history of humans, restaurants are relatively new. The first public restaurant opened in Paris in 1770. It took 70 more years before the first restaurant opened in London, and it was for men only. Not until the late nineteenth century was it thought proper for women to be seen eating in a public restaurant.

Perhaps you have heard the expression: "There is no free lunch."
Well, there used to be. Between roughly 1890 and 1910, men could
get a free lunch at saloons if they bought one or two drinks. So it
wasn't really free, but it must have made a good advertisement.

In the United States, there are more than 300,000 restaurants serving
130 million meals daily.

If you like fast food, you should revere the 1904 St. Louis Exposition.
Many of today's favorite fast foods were introduced to the public there.
Although sausages had been a popular food item for many years, hot
dogs served in buns first gained
popularity at the Exposition.
The public also first tasted
Dr. Pepper soda, ice cream
cones, and hamburgers
at the Exposition. If
you have to do a
history day project
for school, you might
relish investigating
the St. Louis fair.

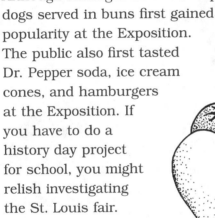

Read the small print.
Have you ever noticed the
patent, trademark, and
copyright marks on food
products? Check them out.
Look at ketchup bottles,
soda cans, and any other
human-made products. Most
product names bear a small "r"
in a circle, like this ®, after the
name. This symbol tells you that
the company registered the name
as a trademark. If you tried to use
the same name for a product, the

company that owned the trademark could sue you. Notice that Pepsi displays the "r" differently than just about any other company. Pepsi puts the symbol after the second "p" in Pepsi. The company thinks it looks better there.

You might see some product names with the letters "TM." The TM stands for "trademark." Companies use TM to tell you that they have not yet registered the trademark, but they are probably in the process of registering it.

On the labels of some products you can find the letter "u" in a small circle. This symbol signifies that the food product is kosher; the product conforms to Jewish dietary laws. Some companies use a lowercase "k" to denote kosher.

On some products you might find a patent number. When you find one, you know that the company has filed a patent for the product or the container. If someone else copied the product, the owner of the patent could sue that person. Patents are numbered in order. George Washington signed patent #1. Today, well over 5 million products have been patented. If a product

has a patent number larger than 5 million, it is a recent invention.

Don't try this at home. During the Renaissance, guests used table runners or cloths to clean their hands. Napkins had not been invented, so people used tablecloths.

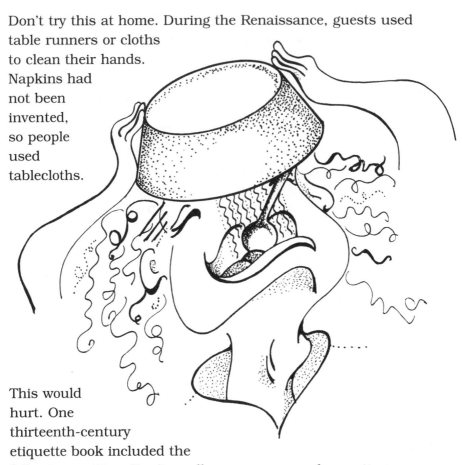

This would hurt. One thirteenth-century etiquette book included the following caution: Don't swallow your spoon when eating soup.

Impress your boyfriend? In Victorian England, a young lady would eat in her room before attending a banquet. That way, she would impress everyone with how little she ate and drank.

Chocolate milk was invented in 1875. What did kids do before that?

No wonder it's taking so long. In case you ordered a boiled ostrich egg, it takes four hours to boil one. Maybe it's not too late to change your order.

Clean your plate. Nearly 20% of all food in the United States is thrown away by restaurants and grocery stores.

Grab the check. How are you going to pay for this meal? If you are planning on using a credit card, thank Frank McNamara for inventing credit cards. Frank made the mistake of taking clients out to dinner one night in 1950 and forgetting his cash. He managed to convince the restaurant staff that he would pay them later, and the experience gave him the idea of establishing a credit system. Along with some other business people, Frank created the first multipurpose credit card, Diners Club.

Breakfast

Pancakes You would have to get up very early in the morning of civilization to beat the Egyptians. They cooked wheat flour patties on stones heated in fires. They were cooking pancakes long before they started baking bread around 2600 B.C. Other cultures also invented their own forms of pancakes.

The *Guinness Book of World Records* shows that the largest pancake ever made was 30 feet across and 1 inch thick. Members of the Lefaivre Lions Club (Ontario, Canada) made and flipped the 1-ton pancake in 1988.

Doughnuts The Dutch are credited with being the first to fry batter in deep fat. Pilgrims brought doughnuts to America in the early seventeenth century. The doughnuts they made were about the size of a walnut, which is the origin of the name, "dough nut." These early doughnuts didn't have a hole in the center. Several Americans figured out that the batter would cook faster if the center were hollowed out. To commemorate this innovation in breakfast foods, people in Rockport, Maine, erected a plaque and dedicated it to the father of the hole in doughnuts, Hanson Gregory.

Milk You think you work hard? It takes an average of 345 squirts from a cow's udder to make a gallon of milk. No wonder they moo all day.

Cereal W.K. Kellogg and his brother, Dr. Harvey Kellogg, invented the process of making cereal flakes in Battle Creek, Michigan. W.K. went on to invent "corn flakes" and to start the Kellogg's Cereal Company in 1906. Charles W. Post, also of Battle Creek, tried the Kellogg's invention and liked it. So Post created his own cereals. First he invented a hot cereal, Postum. Later he created a cold cereal, Grape Nuts. Both Post and Kellogg's companies became huge successes. In 1930, K.W. Kellogg established the Kellogg Foundation, which is one of America's largest philanthropic foundations.

Lunch and dinner

Hot dogs The food we know today as hot dogs was developed in Frankfurt, Germany, in 1852. Like other sausages of the day, hot dogs took on the name of the region where they originated. People called them Frankfurters.

Although it seems inescapable that hot dogs would be served in buns, it took people nearly 50 years to come up with that idea. It wasn't until 1900 that Harry Stevens first served a grilled frank on a split bun. The St. Louis Exposition in 1904 exposed the public to this food innovation and made hot dogs a popular American meal.

At some point people started calling hot dogs by the nickname of "dachshund sausage," because of the similarities in shape. The name "hot dogs" was applied to frankfurters for the first time in 1906 by a sports cartoonist. The cartoonist was watching vendors selling "red-hot" sausages at a baseball game, and he was inspired to draw a cartoon of a dachshund dog in a bun. Unable to spell "dachshund," he labeled the food a hot dog. And the name stuck.

The Coney Island Chamber of Commerce didn't like the name "hot dogs." They banned the use of that name and directed their businesses to call them "Coney Dogs."

Whatever you call them, we eat a lot of them in the United States. The annual consumption in America is about 18 billion hot dogs.

Hamburgers The cooks of Hamburg, Germany, weren't the first to serve chopped or shredded beef. However, they used their own recipe of spices and gave the popular food its name.

Not everyone agrees with this origin for the name hamburger. The citizens of Hamburg, New York, argue that this meal on a bun originated there. They claim, and they might be correct, that two American brothers, Charles and Frank Menches, invented the burger on a bun in 1885. That would make this all-American meal truly an all-American meal.

That first hamburger served under the golden arches of a McDonald's restaurant was made by Maurice and Richard McDonald in Pasadena, California, in 1948.

Salisbury steak Dr. Salisbury, an English physician, recommended that food be chopped into small pieces to aid digestion. We remember his contribution to food science by using his name to designate chopped steak, the Salisbury steak.

Ketchup Ketchup is a word derived from Chinese meaning "pickled-fish-brine or sauce." There are several spellings of the name, and originally ketchup contained no tomato sauce. Centuries passed after the introduction of ketchup to Europe before American sailors added tomatoes to the mixture around 1790. Note that the ketchup bottle on your table probably says "tomato ketchup." What would happen today if you found a pickled fish brine in your ketchup bottle?

Henry Heinz was the first to make ketchup commercially. He started in the late nineteenth century. His ketchup was one of his "57" varieties of products. He selected the number 57, not because he had 57 products, but because he liked that number. By the time he decided to use "57 varieties," his company already was producing more than 57 products.

French fries aren't French This style of frying potatoes originated in Belgium, not France. However, this method of cooking potatoes spread to France from neighboring Belgium, and from there to America. Americans probably didn't know about the Belgium origin when they started calling the fried potatoes French fries. Today, nearly a quarter of the entire potato crop in America is used to make French fries.

Spaghetti
Spaghetti was invented in China thousands of years before it was introduced to Italians. In Italian, spaghetti means "little strips, strands, or cords."

Pizza Have you noticed how many foods were invented in China? Well, here's one food the Chinese didn't invent: pizza. The Greeks did. Actually, several groups can lay claim to the concept, but Greeks were the first to bake toppings on bread. The edges of the bread served as handles to hold the pizza while eating, and the bread itself served as a plate. The pizza shell served as the baking tray, the plate, and the base to hold all the other ingredients. And the best part was having nothing left to wash after a meal.

The word "pizza" comes from a Latin word used to describe a black, tarlike coating. This yucky coating came from the ash created by wood fire. Imagine how sales of pizza would drop today if they were covered by a black layer of ash. Or imagine how unsuccessful a pizza chain would be if it named itself the "Tar-Coated Pie."

Tomatoes weren't added to pizza until the mid sixteenth century when Spanish explorers brought tomatoes and other new-world vegetables to Europe.

America's first pizza parlor was opened in New York in 1905 by Gennaro Lombardi. It took many years before pizza became popular, but today Americans eat the equivalent of about 100 acres of pizza each day. There are well over 50,000 pizzerias in America.

In case you are ordering a pizza at home, instead of going out to eat, consider these findings from a survey conducted a few years ago. According to the survey conducted for Domino's Pizza, if people telephone order pizza while watching newscasts, they are most likely to do it during the weather segment. Also, Domino's Pizza reports, when the pizza arrives at their door, most people answer the door barefoot. There is a correlation between the length of the driveway and the size of the tip. The longer the driveway, the smaller the tip. And women give larger tips than men.

Tabasco Sauce That bottle of Tabasco Sauce on the restaurant table has a heritage reaching back to the Civil War. Edmund McIhenney and his family were forced off their island, Avery Island, Louisiana, by Union Troops. When they returned after the war, they found their home and business ruined. The only thing of value they had was a successful crop of capsicum hot peppers. Edmund mixed up the peppers into a sauce and bottled it in discarded cologne bottles. He gave this first batch of Tabasco Sauce to his friends. They liked it and asked for more. Soon he was producing thousands of bottles each year, and he was on his way to establishing a prosperous business.

Soda pop The soda pop business got its start when Joseph Priestley discovered that he could capture bubbles of carbon dioxide gas in water. He was conducting experiments with gas that formed above a vat of brewing beer. During one experiment, he dropped chemicals into the vat, ruining the beer. This incident ended his experiments because the brewers tossed him out. However, Priestley continued to make soda water, or water with carbon dioxide, and became famous for it. Today we are more likely to remember Joseph Priestley as the scientist who discovered oxygen.

Peanuts How's your peanut sandwich? Over half the peanuts consumed in the United States are eaten as peanut butter. One acre of peanuts can make 30,000 peanut butter sandwiches.

George Washington Carver discovered over 300 uses of peanuts, but he did not invent peanut butter. W.K. Kellogg, the man who started the giant Kellogg cereal company, invented peanut butter. Kellogg also invented corn flakes and started the breakfast cold cereal industry.

If you like honey on your peanut butter sandwich, consider the work that goes into making the honey. It takes bees about 4,200 trips between the nest and flowers to make a tablespoon of honey. Eat slowly so you can enjoy the work of the busy bees.

Snacks

Graham crackers Graham crackers are named after Reverend Sylvester Graham. Rev. Graham advocated eating only unprocessed flours and homemade breads and cereals. Graham crackers are made from unprocessed wheat flour, which is called Graham flour. Another food pioneer, Dr. James Jackson, invented granola and named it after Rev. Graham.

Potato chips George Crum, Chef of the Moon Lake Lodge in Saratoga, New York, invented potato chips by accident in 1890. He was tired of hearing the complaints of a customer who thought Crum's fried potatoes were too soggy. So Crum sliced a potato paper thin, fried it to a crisp, and salted it heavily. He thought the customer wouldn't like this chip either, but at least it would stop him from complaining. To his surprise, the patron loved the chip. So George started making Saratoga Chips, and others copied him. Some time later, people stopped calling them Saratoga Chips and started calling them potato chips. Today, 80% of the U.S. potato harvest goes to making potato chips, French fries, or other processed foods.

Much of the popularity of potato chips is the result of tireless marketing by Herman Lay. His brand of potato chips was the first to be sold coast to coast. In 1961 he merged his company with the Frito Company to create Frito-Lay.

Pretzels Pretzels were first made as a reward for religious studies. An Italian monk made pretzels to give as rewards to children who memorized their prayers. The name pretzel comes from a Latin word that means reward. The shape was to meant to signify a child praying, with hands folded together.

Desserts

Take it away The word "dessert" comes from French, meaning "to clear away," as in clear away the dishes from the meal before we have the sweet stuff at the end.

Toll House cookies America's favorite type of cookie, chocolate chip, was invented by mistake. Ruth Ann Wakefield always made her favorite chocolate cookies by melting chocolate and mixing it in with the batter. However, one day when she was in a hurry, she decided just to add small chunks of chocolate, without melting them, to the batter. She expected the chocolate to melt and mix with the batter while baking. However, the chocolate didn't mix. Her mistake created a new type of cookie. Since Mrs. Wakefield and her husband, Ken, owned the Toll House Inn, the cookies became known as Toll House Cookies.

It took several years, but eventually Nestle figured out that they could sell lots of their semisweet chocolate if they made it into chips or morsels. They bought the name "Toll House" from the Wakefields in 1940 and began printing it, along with Mrs. Wakefield's recipe, on their bags of chocolate chips. The name and recipe are still there today.

In America, chocolate chip, or Toll House, cookies outsell all other kinds. By one estimate, we make over 7 billion of them. That's enough cookies to stretch around the world nine times. Thank you, Mrs. Wakefield.

Fig Newtons Fig Newtons were created after James Mitchell had invented a machine but didn't know what to make with it. His machine, invented in 1892, made an empty shell out of cookie dough. He searched for a filling to put into his extruded dough. People at Kennedy Biscuit Works suggested using fig jam. He tried it, and everyone liked the new product. But no one had a good name for the new cookie. They wanted "fig" in the name. They also wanted the name to include some reference to their region of New England. They thought about "Fig Boston" for a name before settling on Fig Newton. Newton is a town in Massachusetts, just outside of Boston.

Ice cream Ice cream is big business in the United States. We produce nearly a billion gallons of it each year. That's enough ice cream for everyone in America to have four gallons. Are you eating your share?

Here is a quick trivia test for everyone at your table. What is America's favorite flavor of ice cream? Although chocolate seems to be the favorite when people are ordering ice cream, lots more vanilla is sold each year. Vanilla accounts for one-third of all the ice cream made in this country.

If you have made ice cream at home, you know how hard you have to work. There are two problems to be overcome in the process: getting the ice cream mixture cold enough, and keeping ice crystals from forming in the ice cream. When you make ice cream at home in an ice cream freezer, you add lots of salt to the ice in the bucket surrounding the ice cream. The salt lowers the freezing point of ice, making the mixture colder and cooling the ice cream more rapidly.

As the ice cream freezes, you have to turn the mixture constantly. When you turn, or churn, the paddle inside the container, you are stirring up the mixture and preventing ice crystals from forming.

The widespread use of ice cream is a recent development. It is a tribute to human technological prowess that you can eat a bowl of it any time you want. Here is a short history of ice cream.

- 2000 B.C. You guessed it, the Chinese invented ice cream, or something similar to ice cream. Anyway, they got the human race started on the concept of freezing milk products.

- 1295 A.D. Right again, Marco Polo brought it to Europe. Remember that the correct answers to nearly every "who invented it" and "who brought it to Europe" questions are the Chinese and Marco Polo. No one knows for sure if old Marco was responsible, but he probably was. And his name is easy to remember.

- Circa 1560. Blasius Villafranca, a name hard to remember, discovered that adding salt reduced the freezing point of liquids, thus opening the way for quicker freezing of ice cream.

- 1770. Francesco Procopio opened the first cafe in Paris. Besides being the first cafe, this business was the first to sell ice cream to the public.

- 1843. Nancy Johnson invented the ice cream freezer. Although improvements have been made, her basic invention is what you use today when you make ice cream at home. However, Nancy didn't patent the freezer. William G. Young patented her design in 1848, U.S. Patent #3254. Young acknowledged that Nancy had invented the freezer. However, he didn't share his patent royalties with her.

- 1856. The first commercial ice cream plant opened in Washington, D.C.

- 1865. The first artificial ice plant was opened. Now ice could be made throughout the year. Before this, ice blocks were cut from lake and river ice in the winter and stored in ice houses.

- 1874. The invention of the ice cream soda. Robert M. Green ran out of cream for a drink he was selling. When he substituted vanilla ice cream for the cream, his sales took off. He had invented the ice cream soda.

- Circa 1900. The ice cream sundae was invented. Supposedly because drinking soda, including ice cream sodas, was outlawed on Sundays, someone created the sundae by combining ice cream and toppings and leaving out the soda. Since the treat was served on Sundays, the name sundae was used to describe it.

- 1919. Christian Nelson invented the I-Scream Bar. He was inspired when a young customer couldn't decide whether to order a dish of ice cream or a chocolate bar. He thought that no one should have to make such a tough decision, so he developed a method of coating ice cream with a layer of chocolate. Russell Stover, who worked for Nelson, suggested changing the name to Eskimo Pie. By 1922 Stover and Nelson were selling over a million Eskimo Pies a day.

- Circa 1920. The Good Humor Sucker, vanilla ice cream covered with a layer of chocolate and frozen on a stick, was invented by Harry Burt of Youngstown, Ohio.

- 1925. Dixie Cups were created. For a nickel you could buy 2½ ounces of ice cream in a paper cup. The inventor, Hugh Moore, copied the name "Dixie" from the business adjacent to his. That was the Dixie Doll Company in New York.
- 1929. Clarence Vogt patented a continuous freezer. Prior to Vogt's invention, ice cream was made in batches. Continuous freezing of ice cream improved the output and efficiency of commercial ice cream manufacturing.
- 1900. Ice was replaced as the coolant for making ice cream. A refrigeration system, using ammonia as the coolant, was invented.
- 1903. The first patent was issued for a mold to make ice cream cones.
- 1904. The ice cream cone became popular at the St. Louis World's Fair. Of course, it had to be at the 1904 St. Louis World's Fair.
- 1939. The first dual compartment refrigerators were made. This allowed people to keep ice cream at home in a freezer. Trying to keep it in a refrigerator before separate compartments were invented resulted in soggy ice cream.
- 1940. The first Dairy Queen opened. It featured soft-serve ice cream, which was made by a new machine that made ice cream in the store.
- 1960. The first fully automatic system for making ice cream was installed.

- _____ (Fill in the blank.) You had your first ice cream cone.

Leftovers

Romans were probably the first people to use doggy bags to take food home. But let's face it, their dogs didn't fare any better than today's do. When going to a banquet at someone's home, Romans carried a "mappa," a linen bag. They used it both as a napkin and as a bag to carry their favorite foods home.

It wasn't too many years ago that restaurants would supply customers with a doggy bag to take home the food they couldn't eat at a restaurant. Today the restaurant staff might give you a piece of aluminum foil to wrap up leftovers. If they bring a piece of aluminum foil to your table, take a look at it. Better look before someone uses it to wrap up the pizza.

With something as thin as aluminum foil, you might expect that both surfaces would be identical. But they aren't. Why is one side shiny and the other side dull?

The shiny side results from the manufacturing process. Aluminum foil is made by squeezing aluminum between rollers. Each pair of rollers squeezes the foil to a thinner dimension. On the final squeeze, two sheets are squeezed through at the same time. One side of each sheet rolls on the polished roller and takes on a shiny luster. The inside surfaces of both sheets contact each other and come out with a less shiny surface.

When you wrap up the leftovers, should the shiny side be on the outside or inside? For a question of such universal importance, you might ask everyone at the table to contribute his or her ideas.

The most important consideration is that the shiny side of the aluminum foil reflects heat more effectively. Thus, to keep hot foods warm, you would fold the shiny side in. To keep cold foods cold, you would do the opposite, since you are trying to keep out the heat.

To test this theory, I tried an experiment. I put two sets of four ice cubes in identically sized squares of aluminum foil. One had the shiny side in, and the other had the shiny side out. I checked them several times and eventually opened them to find that the cubes with the shiny side out melted noticeably slower than the other. There really is a difference in the two sides of aluminum foil. My experiment was not rigorously scientific, but it was fun. You might try a similar experiment on your way home from the restaurant.

When you take the leftovers home, you put them into the refrigerator. The modern refrigerator was first put on the market in 1913 in Chicago. Before that, home refrigerators were iceboxes, which required a daily supply of ice to keep food cold. But ice can't keep food frozen, so it wasn't until refrigerators had separate freezer sections that frozen food became possible. Up to 1930, Americans bought more iceboxes than refrigerators. But in that year, refrigerators became the established appliance for keeping food. By 1944, nearly 70% of the homes in America had mechanical refrigerators. With home refrigerators and freezers, Clarence Birdseye's invention became popular. In 1924, Birdseye invented processes for fast-freezing food.

He obtained 168 patents for his inventions. Of course, maybe it is the thought of one more frozen dinner that has propelled you to a restaurant tonight. Whether at home or at a restaurant, thank Clarence Birdseye for your meal.

Bibliography

Bohren, Craig F. *Clouds in a Glass of Beer, Simple Experiments in Atmospheric Physics.* New York: John Wiley & Sons, Inc., 1987.

Burke, James. *Connections.* Boston: Little, Brown and Company, 1978.

Caney, Steven. *Invention Book.* New York: Workman Publishing, 1985.

Feldman, David. *Do Penguins Have Knees?* New York: HarperCollins, 1991.

Gardner, Martin. *Entertaining Science Experiments with Everyday Objects.* Mineola, New York, 1981.

Grun, Bernard. *The Timetables of History.* New York: Touchstone, 1982.

Guinness Book of World Records. New York: Bantam Books, 1990.

Inventive Genius. Alexandria, Virginia: Time-Life Books, 1991.

Krensky, Stephen. *Scoop After Scoop. A History of Ice Cream.* New York: Atheneum, 1986.

Lang, George. *Lang's Compendium of Culinary Nonsense and Trivia.* New York: Clarkson N. Potter, Inc., 1980.

Ontario Science Centre. *Foodworks.* Reading, Massachusetts: Addison-Wesley Publishing Company, Inc., 1987.

Panati, Charles. *Panati's Extraordinary Origins of Everyday Things.* New York: Harper & Row, 1987.

Sharp, Arthur G. "Tasteless and Full of Holes." In: *American Heritage of Invention & Technology.* Volume 11, Number 2. Fall 1995.

Slomon, Evelyne. *The Pizza Book.* New York: Times Books, 1984.

Sobey, Ed. *Inventing Stuff.* Palo Alto, California: Dale Seymour Publications, 1995.

Swezey, Kenneth M. *Science Tricks for Fun.* Greenwich, Connecticut: Fawcett Publications, Inc., 1948.

Walker, Jearl. *The Flying Circus of Physics with Answers.* New York: John Wiley & Sons, 1977.

Zubrowski, Bernie. *Messing Around with Drinking Straw Construction.* Boston: Little, Brown, 1981.

Index

A

absorption, napkins and, 61
air pressure, 107-108
atmospheric pressure, 37

B

Birdseye, Clarence, 129
Bohre, Craig, 41
Boston Tea Party, 29
bridges, making out of straws, 19
bubbles, 33-42
    blowing, 8-10
    soda, 35-37
buildings
    making out of straws, 18-19
    making out of toothpicks and peas,
        92-93
Burt, Harry, 126

C

candles, 79-86
    blowing on, 79-81
    extinguishing flame of, 83-86
    production of light from, 82
carbon dioxide, 38-40, 83-84
carbonation, 40
Carver, George Washington, 120
cereal, 114
chocolate milk, 112
coffee, 23-29
    adding creamer to, 27-28
    cooling it, 29
    discovery of, 23
    growing area, 26
    instant, 25
    rings in hot, 24
coins, 95-108
    blowing into a glass, 107-108

coins, *continued*
   copper in, 102
   E Pluribus Unum on, 95
   erupting soda and, 105
   In God We Trust on, 96
   inertia game using, 100-102
   magic trick using, 98-100
   milling edges of, 96-97
   mint date, 96
   nickels, 102
   pennies, 102
   putting in a glass of water, 102-104
   rubbing patterns, 97-98
   silver dollars, 102
   spinner/slider game with, 106-107
combustion, 81
condensation, 42
Coney Island, 115
copyrights, 110
Crum, George, 120

D

Diamond Match Company, 88
Dickens, Charles, 22
doggy bags, 128
doughnuts, 114

E

E Pluribus Unum, 95
Edison, Thomas, 100
eggs, 112
electricity, static, 68-69

F

Fig Newtons, 122-123
fire extinguisher, 83
flute
   history, 4
   straw, 3-8
forks (*see* silverware)
French fries, 117

G

gas, 33
glasses, 71-78
   flipping game using, 71-72
   hearing sound through, 73-74
   measuring, 78
   milk residue on, 75-76
   musical instruments from, 76-77
   seeing through, 74-75
graham crackers, 120
Green, Robert M., 126

H

hamburgers, 116
Heinz, Henry, 117
hot dogs, 115

I

ice cream, 123-127
ice cubes
   crevasses made in by salt, 67
   picking them up with salt, 66
   salt and, 64-65
inertia, 100-102

J

Jackson, Dr. James, 120
Johnson, Nancy, 125

K

ketchup, 116-117
knives (*see* silverware)
kosher, 111

L

leftovers, 128-130
Louisana Purchase Exposition of
   1904, 31

M

Mach 1, 5, 6
magnification, 75
matches, 87-92
  box game, 91-92
  flipping game with, 89-90
  history of, 87
  improvements to, 88
  pickup game with, 88-89
Matthews, John, 34
milk, 114
  chocolate, 112
Mitchell, James, 122
molecules, 5
Morrison, Wade, 35

N

napkins, 59-61
  absorption and, 61
  grease and reflections, 60-61
  history of, 59
Nelson, Christian, 126

O

optical illusions, 51-53
Osborne, Faye, 30
oxygen, 119

P

pancakes, 113
patent numbers, 111
peanuts, 120
Pemberton, Dr. Julian, 34
Pepper, Dr. Charles, 35
pizza, 117-118
placemats, 51-57
  blowing strips of, 55-56
  cutting a hole in, 54-55
  drawing stories on, 56-57
  optical illusions with, 51-53
  squeezing coins through, 53
Polo, Marco, 125
polypropylene, 1
potato chips, 120-121

pressure, atmospheric, 37
pretzels, 121-122
Priestley, Joseph, 33, 119
Procopio, Francesco, 125
projects
  with candles, 79-86
    blowing on, 79-81
    extinguishing flame of, 83-86
  with coffee, 23-29
    adding cream to, 27-28
    cooling it, 29
    instant, 25
    rings in hot, 24
  with coins, 95-108
    blowing into a glass, 107-108
    erupting soda and, 105
    inertia game using, 100-102
    magic trick, 98-100
    putting in a glass of water, 102-104
    rubbing patterns, 97-98
    spinner/slider game with, 106-107
  with glasses, 71-78
    flipping game using, 71-72
    hearing sound through, 73-74
    measuring, 78
    milk residue on, 75-76
    musical instruments from, 76-77
    seeing through, 74-75
  with matches, 87-92
    box game, 91-92
    flipping game, 89-90
    pickup game, 88-89
  with napkins, 59-61
    absorption and, 61
    grease and reflections, 60-61
  with placemats, 51-57
    blowing strips of, 55-56
    cutting a hole in, 54-55
    drawing stories on, 56-57
    optical illusions, 51-53
    squeezing coins through, 53
  with salt, 63-69
    crevasses made in ice cubes by, 67
    ice cubes and, 64-65
    picking up ice cubes with, 66
    picking up salt with a balloon, 68
    taste buds and, 64

projects, *continued*
  with silverware, 43-50
    balancing forks on edge of glass,
      45-46
    making sound using forks, 46-49
    reflections from, 50
    sticking a spoon to your nose, 49
  with soda, 33-42
    bubbling over, 35-37
    observing carbon dioxide in, 38-40
    placing a straw in, 40
    shaking salt in, 41-42
  with straws, 1-22
    blowing up drinks with, 14-16
    constructing billboards with, 19
    constructing bridges with, 19
    constructing buildings with, 18-19
    constructing easels with, 19
    constructing tripods with, 19
    exploding straws, 12-13
    musical instruments, 3-8
    picking up objects using, 14
    rockets, 10-11
    siphons, 16-17
    sound bubbles, 8-10
    sucking up soda with, 18
  with tea, 29-30
  with toothpicks, 92-93

R
reflection, 50, 60-61
restaurants, history, 109-113
rockets, straw, 10-11

S
salisbury steak, 116
salt, 63-69
  adding to soda, 41-42
  crevasses made in ice cubes by, 67
  freezing temperature and, 65
  history of, 63
  ice cubes and, 64-65
  picking up ice cubes with, 66
  picking up with a balloon, 68
  taste buds and, 64

salt water, 37
silverware, 43-50
  balancing forks on edge of glass,
    45-46
  history of, 43-45
  making sound using forks, 46-49
  reflections from, 50
  sticking a spoon to your nose, 49
siphons, 16-17
smoke, 81
soda, 33-42
  bubbling over, 35-37
  carbon dioxide and, 38-40
  Coca-Cola, 34
  Dr. Pepper, 35, 110
  erupting with coins, 105
  history of, 119
  Pepsi, 111
  placing a straw in, 40
  shaking salt in, 41-42
soda water, 33
  discovery of, 33, 34
soft drinks (*see* soda)
sound, 47
  blowin bubble and, 8-10
  hearing through glasses, 73-74
  liquids and, 28
  making with forks, 46-49
  speed of, 5, 6
  tone of, 6
  using glasses as musical
    instruments, 76-77
spaghetti, 117
speed of sound, 5, 6
spoons (*see* silverware)
St. Louis Exposition of 1904, 110, 115
static electricity, 68-69
Stone, Marvin, 2
straws, 1-22
  blowing sound bubbles with, 8-10
  blowing up drinks with, 14-16
  constructing billboards with, 19
  constructing bridges with, 19
  constructing buildings with, 18-19
  constructing easels with, 19
  constructing tripods with, 19
  exploding, 12-13

inventor of, 2
muscial instruments from, 3-8
phrases using the word straw, 22
picking up objects with, 14
placing in soda, 40
rockets from, 10-11
siphoning fluids with, 16-17
sucking up soda with, 18
sugar, taste buds and, 64
Sullivan, Thomas, 30

T

tabasco sauce, 119
taste buds
salt and, 64
sugar and, 64
tea, 29-30
American consumption of, 29
discovery of, 29
iced, 31
invention of tea bags, 30

temperature
cooling hot coffee, 29
salt and freezing temperature, 65
Toll House cookies, 122
tone, 6, 28
toothpicks, 92-93
trademarks, 110-111

V

Villafranca, Blasius, 125
vision, seeing through glasses, 74-75
Vogt, Clarence, 127

W

Wakefield, Ruth Ann, 122
Walke, John, 87

Y

Young, William G., 125

About the author

Ed Sobey is a museum director, scientist, and adventurer. He has
directed four museums, including the national museum of inventing,
Inventure Place, Akron, Ohio. With a Ph.D. in oceanography from
Oregon State University, he has participated in expeditions to
Antarctica, Alaska, South America, the Bahamas, and across the
Pacific Ocean in a sailboat. In 1981 he became a Fellow in the
Explorers Club.

Sobey produces his own television program for kids on inventing and
creativity, the "Idea Factory," which appears weekly on KFSN-ABC in
Fresno. He is on the faculty at California State University, Fresno.

With his wife and two sons, Ed developed many of the activities in
this book while waiting at restaurants for their dinner to be served.
Wrapper Rockets and Trombone Straws is Ed's fifth book.